STAND BY ME

STAND BY ME

Caring for Your Aging or Ailing Dog

Ellen L. Bassuk, M.D.
Julie Santoes
Kate Pittman, D.V.M.

Illustrations by
Christina Ean Spangler

Willow Street Press   New York

CONTENTS

FOREWORD

The symptoms of old age and decline have been steadily creeping up on your beloved dog. It happened slowly, incrementally. So you're a little stunned to find out he has been enduring painful arthritis, severe dental disease, heart disease, or cognitive issues. Maybe your veterinarian has given your dog a life-threatening diagnosis like cancer. You're overwhelmed with worry and panic. What do you do now?

Even more emotionally shocking: your veterinarian suggests that euthanasia is your best option. "It might be time to put him down."

For years, this may have been the only truly humane option. But times are changing. Advances in palliative care for animals and pet hospice programs are opening a new world of healthy options for your beloved pet.

The animal hospice movement is new and only 5% of vet practices even suggest palliative medicine or hospice care for pets at the end of their lives. Millions of dogs are prematurely lost to loving families because pet owners are unaware that there are real alternatives to euthanasia when responding to a diagnosed life limiting condition.

As a pioneer in end-of-life care for geriatric pets – or Pawspice – I urge dog lovers to read this book to learn about

3

your options before agreeing to euthanasia. With a Pawspice program, the primary disease can be managed and symptoms, such as pain or incontinence, are addressed by the pet owner and veterinarian working together as a team.

Stand by Me offers a tremendous amount of practical information for dog lovers to help them decide if they are up for the challenges – and considerable rewards – of providing veterinary supervised palliative medicine and hospice care for their beloved older and ailing pets.

In this book, Ellen Bassuk, M.D. and her co-authors describe their experiences with their own dogs and provide clear guidelines, often not offered by veterinarians, to help you care for your dog at the end of his life.

Palliative and hospice care may restore quality of life and comfort for your beloved dog, prolonging his life and giving your family and your dog precious time for an extended, more comfortable farewell.

Dr. Alice Villalobos is President Emeritus of the Society for Veterinary Medical Ethics, and Fellow Emeritus of the National Academies of Practice. She is the developer of Pawspice for end-of-life pet care.

PREFACE

Stand by Me emerged from our personal experiences with our dogs as they became sick and old. Two of the authors have cared for hundreds of aging and ailing dogs during their professional careers.

Like all dog owners, we love our animals deeply and wish to extend their lives for as long as they can enjoy a reasonable quality of life in their daily experiences. As we cared for our older dogs and began to face the inevitable decline brought on by old age and disease, we looked for resources to help us. There was little to be found.

When a dog is diagnosed with a potentially life-threatening illness, especially if he is already symptomatic, veterinarians commonly suggest immediate euthanasia rather than discussing the possibilities of palliative care. Historically, euthanasia has been the "go to" veterinarian response to disease and old age. Understandably, many dog owners may be reluctant to commit to caring for their dogs at home as they begin to decline and lose their functions. Taking on the challenge of caring for very sick or old dogs can be formidable, even with help and support.

Initially, the severity of your dog's illness can leave you frightened and heartbroken. You may not have the emotional space to think straight or consider an alternative to immediate euthanasia. Shocked and saddened, you may want to go along with the vet's suggestion. We hope this book will create space for you to look past your initial shock and consider the rewards of palliative and hospice care.

Palliative care for aging and ailing dogs is on the rise. Vets increasingly are supporting dog owners who undertake this loving task. Many dogs who are old and sick can be engaged, affectionate, comfortable, and relatively pain free – giving both owner and dog memorable additional time together.

Your relationship with your dog must evolve as your dog's needs change. This last chapter of your dog's life will present challenges, but also precious, unforgettable moments of closeness and contact. You will be giving your dog the kind of love and support that he has always given to you so unselfishly.

You will need new tools to support your dog through the aging and ailing process. You can learn how to enhance your dog's quality of life, to minimize suffering and maximize happy moments. You can learn new skills to prevent or slow the onset of disease and you can develop your own approach to know when it is time to say goodbye. It can be hard to deal with some of the symptoms you will see in your ailing pet but knowing how to manage your dog's decline and ultimate passing can make this less difficult for both of you.

This book is intended as a guide and resource for those who make the choice to stand by their dog until the end. The heartbreaking moment when your dog must finally depart can sometimes be safely delayed for weeks, month or even longer – creating precious time for you to be together. Our aim is to give you the tools to help your dog pass with grace, dignity and comfort. For you, the loving caregiver, our goal is to help you take control of your pet's end of life without fear and with compassion while also facing your own painful feelings.

If you have already made the decision to proceed with palliative care for your dog, this book will guide you. If you are thinking about whether to go forward or not, this book can help you decide.

On behalf of dogs everywhere, we thank you.

Ellen L. Bassuk, M.D.

KAILIE

Hello, old friend. We're here in this most beautiful and familiar place, sharing a quiet moment together. For 15 years, we've been with each other, and now you are close to leaving. I understand all the things I must do to keep you safe, comfortable, and happy until you tell me it's time.

As I sit here with you, I'm taken back to our first meeting. You were a tiny thing, terrified of the noise and bizarre surroundings of the animal shelter. Over the years, we've spent time together in many places, and our shared experience of trauma bound us instantly. Our recovery journey together has covered a lot of ground – from the mountains of northern Nevada to the swamps and bayous on the Texas/Louisiana border. We traveled by car, by horseback, by motorcycle, and always you were there.

Remember the outreach work we did together in Nashville? Your friendliness and crazy terrier face with those wild and bushy eyebrows on that big lab body would instantly disarm and charm the most hardened or fearful person. Thank you for that. So many people would still be alone and suffering if not for you.

Now, it's hard for you to walk because your arthritis is so painful. You no longer chase your ball, but you're still happy to carry it on our nightly walks. There are many things we don't do as much anymore, but we are content just to be in each other's presence. Soon, we're going to close this adventure together. I promised you I'd let you go when it was time and clearly that time is near.

We've walked a recovery journey together for 15 years, and your unconditional love and companionship has been a beautiful addition to a life of ever-increasing joy and stability. I hope I've honored you with the most amazing life a dog could wish for. It goes without saying that I'm going to miss you terribly when you're gone, but it is a sorrow I'll endure with honor and dignity reflecting a life well-lived.

For now, let's just sit here and enjoy the evening. There's a cool breeze picking up, Kailie. Do you feel it?

- Steve S.

PART I
THE JOURNEY AHEAD

Our dogs mean so much to us.

They are our close friends, our loyal and loving family members and our best company when we are feeling down. They are our secret keepers. They seem to know just what we need. Always happy to see us, no matter what mood we're in or how long we've been gone. Their love is always there – no questions asked, nothing asked in return. If we are mad at them or forget to feed them or take them for a walk, they never hold a grudge. They don't judge or criticize. Coming home after a bad day, our stress melts away as we are greeted by a wagging tale on one end and a happy grin on the other.

Dogs protect us. Some give their lives as police dogs, military dogs, or bomb-sniffing dogs at airports. Helping first responders in natural disasters, dogs toil in rescue and recovery with no expectations of payment other than a favorite chew toy or a pat on the head, searching tirelessly for victims who are perfect strangers.

Therapy dogs bring hope and joy to thousands of people every day, visiting elderly people in nursing homes, hospitals, and hospice care. Dogs enrich the lives of children who are sick or in the hospital, so ill that they can't go home. A visit from a dog can brighten their lives and make them forget their pain, even if only for a few minutes.

Dogs are tuned into us on extraordinary and existential levels. Children with autism who have difficulty connecting with other people find ways to communicate with dogs. Dogs can predict seizures and detect low blood sugar levels for people with diabetes. They support people with various physical and mental illnesses to feel safer and go out into the world. Men and woman who serve our country in combat and come home with psychological wounds find ways to heal with the help of a dog.

Dogs can form multiple loving unconditional attachments over their lifetimes. They can offer unconditional love to their primary caregiver and then go on to form strong attachments with other owners later in life. Rescue dogs who may have been traumatized are able to form loving relationships with new owners. Service dogs become devoted to their new charges. It is the quality of the relationship that matters most to a dog.

Dogs don't worry about what will happen tomorrow, or whether we are good enough, or "what will happen if...". Many of us know intellectually that the principle of "living in the moment" is the key to reducing stress and worry – but with all our daily distractions we struggle to put that principle into effect. If we only appreciated how dogs live their lives, we could look to them as a helpful example!

As a nation, we invest more than 60 billion dollars a year on our dogs for food, medical care, dog walkers, doggie day care, boarding, grooming, doggie spas, beds, toys – you name it. But what our dogs give us back can never be measured in dollars. A dog's love is unconditional, without limitation, and complete. Once you've had a dog in your life, it is hard to imagine ever being without one.

They don't ask much of us, do they? But a time may come when your dog most needs your love and support when she is old and slowing down with aches and pains, or sickness and disease. She may need a more comfortable bed or a sweater to warm her from the cold. Caring for her can be hard work. It requires patience when she can't tell you what she needs or where it hurts, or when she's had enough.

DECIDING ABOUT PALLIATIVE AND HOSPICE CARE

When your dog is very old and failing or has been diagnosed with an aggressive cancer or other serious illness, euthanasia should be part of the discussion – but not the entire discussion. Other options for continued care should also be discussed. These should be considered in light of your dog's level of pain, suffering, and overall quality of life, as well as your willingness and ability to provide adequate care to prolong her life.

Palliative and hospice care in your home with support from your vet can be an alternative to euthanasia. This approach seeks to comfort and support rather than to cure – to control and mitigate pain, maximize comfort, and support and enhance the time that is left. This can provide support to both you and your dog.

> *"Hospice is the philosophy of care that regards death as a natural process, prioritizes comfort and quality of life over quantity of life as death draws near and supports the cultural and spiritual aspects of dying. Palliative care, which may be provided at any time over the course of an illness... provides expert pain and symptom relief as well as emotional support and help navigating the healthcare system for patients and families. Hospice, simply defined, is palliative care at the end of life."*
>
> Katherine J. Goldberg, DVM

Only recently has palliative care become an option in caring for seriously ill animals. Alice Villalobos, DVM, FNAP, a pioneer in palliative and hospice care for animals, has developed "Pawspice," an approach that maximizes quality of life (QOL) as an alternative to euthanasia or aggressive treatment in seriously ill or terminally ill animals. "Pawspice embraces both palliative and kinder, gentler forms of standard care to treat serious oncologic disease," Dr. Villalobos writes. "Pawspice transitions to hospice (comfort care) as the patient's decline approaches the final weeks, days or hours of life."

The Pawspice approach is focused on minimizing pain and optimizing the dog's comfort and quality of life – and knowing when the balance shifts. For example, with cancer, Pawspice uses low-toxicity chemotherapy in modified protocols along with immunonutrition. Family members focus on managing symptoms and maximizing the dog's comfort.

Dr. Villalobos suggests implementing palliative care as soon as the diagnosis is made rather than waiting until the animal is very close to the end of life. This is a proactive treatment that minimizes pain and suffering and increases care and comfort. It is a strategy for increasing the quality of life for as long as possible, rather than just a response to impending death.

A palliative care plan can be developed, led, and coordinated by your veterinarian – ideally one who is a hospice-oriented veterinarian. To help your dog you may need to learn new skills such as how to administer medication and subcutaneous fluids, and how to identify and treat pain. You might use alternative therapeutic approaches or take advantage of emotional supports such as pet bereavement groups or counseling. Most importantly for you and your dog, you will maximize the time you have left together.

COMPLEMENTARY AND ALTERNATIVE MEDICINES

When seeking comfort for your ailing dog, alternative approaches can complement the care your vet prescribes. Alternative treatments should be reviewed and understood by your vet before used in tandem with traditional treatments. Many complementary and alternative medicine (CAM) treatments are consistent with the principles of palliative care.

Evidence for the effectiveness of these treatments is not conclusive, although emerging studies as well as our experience suggest they may help your pet feel better. It is important to consider the potential advantages, as well as possible adverse effects of these approaches (which, on the whole, are minimal) and discuss them with your vet.

Alternative treatments are generally non-toxic and can improve the well-being of your dog by promoting the body's ability to heal. Humans have increasingly used these approaches to support their own health and healing; it is estimated that more than one-third of adults use some type of

CAM in their own health care. Why shouldn't the dog enjoy the same alternative medicine care as the owner?

Popular CAM treatments include:

- o **Acupuncture.** An age-old Chinese treatment in which small-gauge needles are inserted in meridians or energy channels (nerve endings and blood vessels) to address issues such as pain, arthritis, nerve damage, chronic respiratory problems, cardiac disorders, and seizures. Acupuncture stimulates the release of the body's anti-inflammatory and pain-relieving substances.

- o **Massage and acupressure.** Both focus on soft tissues, including muscles. This may especially help dogs after a surgical procedure and dogs with arthritis. Most dogs love being touched, so your dog will probably enjoy receiving this hands-on therapy.

- o **Cold Laser Therapy.** Low level laser therapy promotes pain relief and healing. Light energy from a hand-held device passes through your dog's skin and has a healing effect on damaged cells.

- o **Physical therapy.** This comprehensive treatment is aimed at controlling pain and maintaining flexibility and movement.

- o **Water therapy.** This includes the use of a treadmill in water and indoor swimming or walking in water. Just as with humans, this can help dogs with joint or spine issues.

- o **Chiropractic care.** Focused on the musculoskeletal system, especially the spine, this may help dogs with back pain, weakness in the hind quarters, muscle spasms, or inflexibility and stiffness.

MANAGING FINANCIAL COSTS

When we take a dog into our life, routine expenses come with him. Food, doggie treats, a leash, routine medical care – let's face it, they don't ask for much. But when your dog is very ill or very old, specialty veterinary care, diagnostic and follow-up procedures, medications, and various supportive devices may be required. We know how costly pet care can be, especially when an ailing dog requires long-term special maintenance.

In this book, we suggest various foods, medications, supports, and treatments – some of which are costly. We have tried to suggest less expensive alternatives when possible. Attention from a veterinarian has a price tag and costs can pile up. As you consider palliative or hospice care in your home, you need to consider the impact on your finances. If you have limited resources, it is important to discuss this with your vet to explore cost-effective ways to manage your dog's condition.

One smart way to handle this is to establish a special dog care fund in which resources are set aside before they are needed. Along with meeting routine medical care costs, you can contribute regular amounts to pay for serious illness or emergencies when they arise. Budgeting ahead of time for your older dog's needs can significantly help ease the cost of care sticker shock.

Pet insurance is another option. Just like with humans, a good insurance plan can go a long way towards easing the financial burden of health care. Be aware that, just like with human plans, the coverage and costs vary considerably. Pet insurance plans have terms and conditions that should be investigated carefully. Do your due diligence as some insurance plans don't cover pre-existing conditions or do not pay the costs directly to the vet. Some plans may have a waiting period before you are reimbursed, and payment may be only partial. Petinsurancereview.com is a helpful consumer-oriented website that reviews insurance plans.

Another helpful resource is CareCredit, Inc. They offer financing for medical care, including veterinary care. They provide a credit card that can be used at your vet clinic to pay for approved care. This financing company offers time-limited, interest-free loans to selected applicants. Of course, if loans are not repaid on time, interest will accumulate and can become expensive, so remember to budget ahead of time for your dog's needs.

Some dog owners use online fundraising sites such as gofundme.com, youcaring.com, or giveforward.com. Most of these websites provide a section specifically for people who need funds to meet their pet's medical expenses. To be successful, you will need to invest significant time and energy into creating, updating and promoting your pet's fundraising appeal.

As you choose the resource that is right for you, remember advance planning and budgeting is vital, just as it is when planning for the care of our elderly parents – or our own care as we grow older. With a little planning and a modest budget, we can avoid having to make "crisis decisions" in the veterinarian's office. A calm, methodical approach to our dog's elder years can help us make better, clearer choices.

A few organizations provide funding to owners who cannot afford medical costs. For example, see www.bestfriends.org in the Resource list below.

RESOURCES

Palliative and Hospice Care

o American Society for the Prevention of Cruelty to Animals. (n.d.). End of life care. *American Society for the Prevention of Cruelty to Animals.* www.aspca.org/pet-care/general-pet-care/end-life-care

o Bishop, G., Cooney, K., Cox, S., Downing, R., Mitchener, K., Shanan, A., ... Wynn, T. (2016). AAHA/IAAHPC end-of-life care guidelines. *American Animal Hospital Association.* www.aaha.org/professional/resources/end_of_life_care_guidelines.aspx

o Hancock, G. (2010). End of life hospice care. *American Association of Human-Animal Bond Veterinarians.* www.aahabv.org/end-of-life-hospice-care

o Lap of Love. (n.d.). Hospice. *Lap of Love.* www.lapoflove.com/Services/Veterinary-Hospice

o Villalobos, A.E. (2011). End-of-life care. *Clinician's Brief.* www.cliniciansbrief.com/article/end-life-care

o Villalobos, A.E. (2017). Quality of life to the end of life: We owe it to them. *The Latham Letter, 38*(1), 8-11. Retrieved from: www.latham.org/Issues/LL_17_WI.pdf#page=8

Complementary and Alternative Medicines (CAM)

o American Academy of Veterinary Acupuncture. Available at: www.aava.org

o International Veterinary Acupuncture Society. Available at: www.ivas.org

o NBCAAM *Animal* Acupressure & *Massage* Practitioners. Available at: www.nbcaam.org

o Handicapped Pet Physical Therapy: www.handicappedpets.com/physical-therapy-for-pet-paralysis

o Chiropractic Therapy. Available at: www.organic-pet-digest.com/dog-chiropractic.html

Managing Financial Costs

o Pet Insurance. Available at www.petinsurancereview.com and www.consumersadvocate.org/pet-insurance

o CareCredit, Inc. Available at: www.carecredit.com/vetmed

o On-profit grant assistance: www.bestfriends.org/resources/general-pet--care/financial-aid-pets

CASSIE

I adopted Cassie when she was five. She was in my life for 12 years. As I watched her grow old, I promised her that she wouldn't suffer when it was time to let her go.

At first, she could no longer jump up on the bed. Then, she stopped climbing the stairs of the front porch. Eventually she didn't want to walk any further than the end of the street. She still enjoyed her food, but her bladder didn't hold as much as it used to. Through all of this, she was still happy and not in too much pain.

One day, Cassie suddenly developed vertigo. She began to wander in circles and then fall over. I could see panic in her eyes. She wasn't eating. I thought her time had come and made an appointment with our vet. But there was good news! Vertigo sometimes afflicts older dogs, but it can go away in a week. I gave her anti-nausea medicine to make sure she could eat and drink, and not risk dehydration. To my relief, she got better. Her balance was still a little off, but she was happy. Her eyes said, "Not yet."

Six months went by and Cassie again lost her appetite. My dog who never complained and never vocalized any pain, was now whining. Her legs kept going out from underneath her. Her bladder was failing while she was lying down. Her eyes now said, "I'm tired. I hurt. It's time."

It was Saturday. My vet is closed on Sundays. I planned to go in on Monday, but there was a snowstorm. Everything was shut down until Tuesday. I spent two days by Cassie's side, telling her how special she was, and how grateful I was to have had her in our lives. On Sunday night, we had steak together. On Monday, I ordered pizza. And on Tuesday, while the vet gave her the injection, I fed her hot dogs. As she slipped away, she was at peace, no longer in pain.

I've had no regrets, no second guesses. No "what-ifs." It was time. I know I did the right thing even though saying goodbye was heart-wrenching. I will always aspire to be as good as Cassie thought I was.

—Kim N.

DOGS AGE DIFFERENTLY

Dogs age more quickly than humans. We've all heard the age-old rule of thumb: one "dog year" equals seven human years. However, we now know this is actually a more complicated calculation.

In fact, dogs of different sizes and breeds age at different rates. Generally, larger dogs age at an accelerated rate compared to smaller dogs. Also, dogs age more rapidly at some stages of their life, depending on their general condition, breed and genetics.

Opinions differ on when a dog is considered a senior. Approximately 40 percent of domestic dogs in the U.S. are 7 years or older. This is often considered to be the beginning of the senior period, depending on the size of the dog. This means an estimated 27 million dogs in the U.S. are in their geriatric years.

The American Animal Hospital Association (AAHA) offers guidelines for classifying dogs as "senior" to promote early detection of disease, prevent or delay illness, manage pain, and provide a framework for evaluating quality of life and end-of-life decisions.

According to these guidelines, your dog can be considered "senior" at the beginning of the last 25 percent of his expected lifespan: around 10 years old for dogs up to 20 pounds; 9 years old for dogs from 21 to 90 pounds; and 7 years old for those over 90 pounds. The chart that follows (adapted from 2017 WebMD data) provides additional estimates of your dog's equivalent age in human years. It will help you gauge your dog's general stage in life.

Throughout your dog's life, a focus on nutrition, exercise, weight, and dental care will help set the stage for a healthier old age and, perhaps, a longer life. Daily care remains important right to the end of a dog's life, as the routine healthcare of early years transitions to the more intensive care of the later years.

Even when there are critical health conditions, continued attention to everyday health care will increase your dog's comfort and quality of life. If you did not focus on these issues when your dog was young, you can begin now to increase her general comfort as she ages.

SIGNS OF NORMAL AGING

As dogs age, structural body systems and functions decline. As your dog ages into her senior years, be aware of changes in her behavior, functioning, health, weight, energy and comfort. Spotting problems as early as possible will help you alleviate the inevitable impact of aging on your dog. Keep your vet informed of any changes you notice.

Aging for a dog is not that much different than aging in a human. Their muzzles become grey or white, their hair dulls. They slow down, have less energy and burn fewer calories. Their lean body mass and muscle mass decrease, and they are more likely to become overweight. Their nutrient absorption doesn't change significantly compared to younger dogs, but their protein requirement increases.

Older dogs are generally slower. Walks become less brisk because older dogs are not able to use oxygen as efficiently. This can be compounded by osteoarthritis, common in older dogs, which may be very painful. They also become less tolerant of temperature extremes. Almost all senior dogs develop some kind of dental disease due to reduced saliva production and often develop bad "dog breath." Many dogs, especially spayed females, begin to dribble urine.

Some dogs experience cognitive decline, occasionally seeming confused and disoriented. You may find your old dog

How Old is My Dog in Human Years?			
Size of Dog	**Small** 20 lbs or less	**Medium** 21-50 lbs	**Large** More than 50 lbs
Age of Dog	**Age in Human Years**		
1 Year	15	15	15
2	24	24	24
3	28	28	28
4	32	32	32
5	36	36	36
6	40	42	45
7	44	47	50
8	48	51	55
9	52	56	61
10	56	60	66
11	60	65	72
12	64	69	77
13	68	74	82
14	72	78	88
15	76	83	93
16	80	87	120

staring at the wall or unable to recognize things that were once familiar. Some older dogs develop behavioral problems as well, such as separation anxiety, fears and phobias (see chapter on Behavior Changes). Many diseases are more frequent in senior dogs, such as osteoarthritis, cognitive dysfunction, chronic kidney disease, heart related diseases and cancer.

LOSS OF SENSORY INPUT

A decline in sensory perception is common in older dogs. Many become hard of hearing or totally deaf and their sense of smell becomes less acute. You may notice a bluish-gray haziness in your elderly dog's eyes; this is nuclear sclerosis which causes increased density of the lens. Often confused with cataracts, this will not affect your dog's vision. It is part of the normal aging process.

The type and severity of the sensory loss will determine how your dog's functioning may be affected. Many older dogs begin to lose their hearing and eventually become deaf. Some have difficulty seeing. Some may need brighter lights and protection from open staircases or doors. Blind dogs are surprisingly adaptable and can learn how to navigate familiar surroundings. Their sense of smell and taste are the last to decline. If you dog loses interest in eating, try adding tasty ingredients to her food.

Tips for Managing Senior Dogs Who Become Deaf or Blind

- o Take time to adjust to how you relate to your deaf or blind dog

- o Always be patient, calm and kind

- o Speak to a blind dog before touching him

- o Approach a deaf or blind dog from the front

- o Reduce the possibilities of surprising the dog

- o Monitor the dog's response to children

- o Ensure the safety of your dog. Do not allow him to roam freely; protect him from cars, open doors, and staircases

- o Use baby gates to restrict designated areas in your home

- o Acclimate your dog to any changes in environment

- o Keep your dog fenced in or on a leash

○ Use positive reinforcement to train him

○ If your dog is deaf, learn hand commands and teach them to your dog (variants of ASL)

○ Be sure to communicate through reassuring touch

○ Consider herbal relaxants, massage or acupuncture

Many illnesses are more likely to develop in older dogs. Some are life threatening; other are not. All require complete evaluation and treatment by a vet. If your dog develops any of the conditions below, your vet should fully assess him and determine a practical treatment plan.

○ Dental disease (see Hygiene chapter).

○ Osteoarthritis, which can be very painful.

○ Laryngeal paralysis, which may lead to trouble with breathing and changes in your dog's vocal sounds.

○ Cardiovascular disease, a leading cause of death in geriatric dogs (approximately 30% of all older dogs have a cardiac problem).

○ Cancer, accounting for the death of more than half of all dogs older than 10 years.

o Cushing's Syndrome, manifested by decreased energy, increased thirst with excessive urination, and skin and hair changes, often affects dogs who are 8– 10 years old.

o Diabetes which affects about one in two hundred dogs and is manifested by excessive urination, weakness, increased thirst and appetite, and weight loss.

PJ

PJ was a smart, dark chocolate miniature poodle who lived for 17 years. She was the love of my young daughter's life and they did everything together. As PJ got older, she remained feisty and energetic, but had increasing periods of irritability and crotchety behavior.

During a routine exam, our vet found that PJ had serious kidney disease requiring daily subcutaneous hydration. To our surprise, she cooperated well with the treatments, and had good days and bad days. But as her illness worsened, she'd periodically lose her appetite, have bouts of vomiting and seemed generally uncomfortable and out of sorts.

On some days PJ was agitated and found it hard to settle. Our vet told us that PJ probably felt nauseous, so we gave her the anti-vomiting medication Cerenia at the first sign of discomfort. This stopped her agitation and vomiting for about 24 hours and continued to work for the next six months. Then she began to decline. She slept more, was far less energetic, hid under the bed for hours and on some days would pace continuously.

As PJ got sicker, there were more and more days when she refused to eat, and seemed more agitated, despite the medication. Finally, she stopped eating entirely, couldn't sit still and could not be reassured. It was clear that she was very uncomfortable, our treatment regimen was no longer effective and that we would have to consider saying goodbye.

We were very sad to lose this little character, but we have fond memories of her boundless energy, toughness and loving disposition. We miss her tearing around the house and leaping into our laps for cuddles. Most of all, we miss her courageousness and exuberant spirit.

−Sarah A.

PART II
CARING FOR YOUR AGING
OR AILING DOG

As you embark on this last journey with your dog, it is wise to consider the pressures on your family, time, finances, career and social life. Imagine her needs expanding and her demands increasing. Make peace with the level of your commitment, and revisit this regularly to keep your heart open and your energy high. Remember, we all have limitations. It is best to know them beforehand, rather than bump into them unprepared.

As you guide and support your dog through her final days, your relationship with her will gradually change. As she becomes increasingly dependent on you for help with activities vital to her comfort and survival, she needs more of your attention. You may find her becoming needier and more anxious when you leave the room or the house. She may want to stay by your side, day or night. You may have to make adjustments in how you deal with her.

As the demands of an aging or sick dog increase, it's normal to develop mixed feelings about your changing relationship with your dog. It is not easy to see your pet decline – and to have increased demands on your time, energy and finances. Your feelings may be complicated – not all of them loving. Have you done enough or too little? Is your dog suffering? Can you tolerate her discomfort? Do you have the energy and compassion to usher your dog through this final stage?

You may feel guilty that you are not doing enough or are not home with her more often. If your dog becomes incontinent, it can be hard to manage and clean up. You can no longer enjoy long peaceful walks without your dog stumbling or sitting down. Similar to caring for of an elderly parent, you may feel burdened and stressed at times.

Most of all, find time to share special moments with your dog. Although she is aging, changing and declining, she is still your loving companion – who now needs your full support, compassion and care. Maximize these special moments. You will cherish them in the years ahead.

DRINKING AND EATING

One day, your aging or ailing dog may be eating just as well as she has before. The next day, she may be finicky or not eating at all. How can you help encourage your dog to eat and drink, and what should you do if she doesn't?

Here are some simple steps you can take: for dogs with limited mobility, change the location of the food and water bowls so she will have easy access to them. If your dog has difficulty bending down due to arthritis, simply elevate his food and water bowls.

Is your dog a little unsteady on her feet when standing for a long time? Try putting the food and water in shallow bowls placed on the floor – she may be more comfortable sitting or lying down to reach her food and water.

Water is Essential for Your Dog

Like all living things, dogs must have water to live. As usual, offer your dog a good supply of fresh, clean water at mealtimes. Monitor your dog's water intake by checking how much is gone from the water bowl. If your dog is drinking regularly and peeing at reasonable intervals, and her pee is clear, then she is likely to be properly hydrated. If her pee is dark, she's not getting enough water.

What should you do to help your dog to remain fully hydrated if she is eating well but just not drinking enough? Try adding water to her food dish at mealtimes. She'll gobble up the water mixed in with the food and that will help maintain good hydration. You can also add low-sodium chicken, beef, or tuna broth from the supermarket to her water bowl.

Or make your own protein-rich broth by putting a whole chicken in a large pot, covering it with cold water, bringing the pot to a boil and then simmering it lightly for up to two hours. Make sure not to add any seasoning while cooking. When cooled, you can freeze the broth into ice cubes or put it in small containers. You can give it to your dog directly or add it to her water dish.

Remember though, if your dog does not drink any water for a 24-hour period, consult a vet or vet tech. Do not let this go for any longer than 24 hours or there is danger of dehydration. How do you know if your dog is getting dehydrated? Keep an eye out for these symptoms of dehydration:

o Low energy

o Excessive panting

o Dry and pale gums

o Decreased skin elasticity: pull up skin; it should bounce back quickly under normal conditions

o Sunken eyes

o Reduced urine output

If your dog stops drinking water as the result of discomfort or disease, it is possible to hydrate her by injecting fluids just below the skin (subcutaneous injection of fluid). Your vet or vet tech can do this, or your vet can teach you how to do this by yourself at home.

Injecting fluids is a simple procedure that most dogs tolerate well. It's understandable you may feel squeamish at first but with some practice, this can be done with ease.

Maintaining Proper Weight

As your dog grows old, her eating habits may generally stay the same but her caloric requirement may lessen as her activity, energy, and lean body mass decline. It is estimated that an 8-year-old dog may require 20 percent fewer calories than a 1 to 2-year-old dog.

If an older dog slows down, but continues with her usual diet, she will gain weight, which can exacerbate any health condition. Overall, it has been shown that calorie restriction increases a dog's longevity.

Just as with people, the rates of obesity among dogs in the U.S. is growing. An estimated 50 percent of dogs older than 7 years are overweight or obese. Dogs weighing more than 10 to 19 percent of the optimum weight for their breed are considered overweight; those weighing more than 20 percent of the optimum weight are considered obese.

Obesity can compromise a dog's health and decrease his lifespan. It also is a risk factor for osteoarthritis, a painful joint condition that can limit a dog's mobility and quality of life. Even a slight weight gain can affect joint health. Obesity is a preventable cause of illness that should be discussed with your vet.

Dog owners can assess their dog's weight on their own to determine the dog's body condition. Dogs of normal weight have normal body contours. They have bony prominences that can be easily felt but should not be seen, and their intra-abdominal fat should not impede abdominal palpitation.

A weight management program may improve the general condition of an aging dog. Reducing calories and increasing physical activity are essential for weight control. Adding fiber may also help but be sure the fiber doesn't replace essential nutrients. A weight loss program should include a targeted ideal weight, maximum daily caloric intake, and specific foods to meet these requirements.

The American Animal Hospital Association (AAHA) offers these Weight Management Guidelines:

- o Serve age-appropriate food in a measured portion using a measuring cup

- o Ensure consistency of feeding time and amount

- o Feed the dog from her own dish and feed her separately from other pets

- o Give the dog treats, but adjust for the calories in the treats

- o Provide appropriate physical activity consistent with the dog's general condition

These guidelines should be adapted according to your dog's unique needs, which include energy level, metabolism, age, breed, current weight, general body condition, and any medical conditions. Any weight maintenance program should be implemented gradually.

How about if your dog is underweight? If there is no identifiable medical cause, offer your dog different foods in various ways as suggested in this chapter. You can increase the amount of food for an underweight dog by one and a half times the recommended amount. As you do this, monitor your dog's weight to see if it approaches a normal range for her size and breed.

Feeding Your Senior or Ailing Dog

Eating comes naturally to a dog. Healthy senior dogs can digest their food just as well as younger dogs, although some may develop sensitive stomachs and become constipated. There is little evidence to suggest that older dogs require a special diet if the animal is eating enough to maintain his weight. However, an older dog's diet should have more protein because of decreased energy intake.

Healthy older dogs can receive an adult maintenance diet without other changes in food that may be needed for senior dogs with health conditions. A standard adult maintenance diet should meet their specific needs for vitamins and minerals. Approximately 25% of a senior dog's diet should come from high quality protein to support protein turnover that occurs as dogs age.

How to Choose Commercial Food for Your Senior Dog:

- A specific meat source is listed (e.g., chicken)

- o Fruits and vegetables are included

- o Oats and barley are included

- o Sunflower oil provides omega-6 essential fatty acids

- o Flaxseed oil or marine fish provides omega-3 acid that may help with brain aging

- o Glucosamine and/or chondroitin may help arthritic dogs

- o Avoid foods with artificial preservatives, mill-run grains, artificial dyes, and those with corn, wheat or soybeans

Some vets suggest that elderly dogs should be transitioned slowly to high protein/high fiber commercial dog food specially developed for senior dogs. These are available as both kibble and canned food. Dogs generally prefer canned food, which is somewhat more expensive but has more water. It is often tastier and easier to chew, especially for dogs with dental disease. You can also mix the two.

Older dogs, even in the pink of health, may react to even a small change in diet. A very old or ailing dog may have a very sensitive gastrointestinal (GI) system that can cause her discomfort or indigestion. Foods to avoid because they are toxic to dogs include chocolate, alcohol, grapes and raisins, macadamia nuts, onions, garlic and the sweetener Xylitol.

Understanding Dog Food Labels

Pet food labels are regulated to provide adequate nutritional information. Food labels must include:

- Product or brand name

- Name and address of manufacturer

- Net weight

- List of ingredients by weight

- Guaranteed analysis of crude protein, crude fat, crude fiber and moisture

- Statement about the method used to ensure nutritional adequacy

Definition of Labeling Terms

- Complete and Balanced: contains required amount and proportion of required nutrients for all life stages

- Limited-Only: limited ingredients applicable to a specific life stage (e.g., adult maintenance)

- Intermittent or Supplemental: food is not balanced and should not be used for extended periods o Therapeutic: only for a specific issue

If your dog stops eating, it is a clear sign that something is wrong. Often, this is not serious and will clear up within 24 hours. If your dog is eating something once or twice a day, and is pooping at least once a day without diarrhea, then she is probably doing OK.

If your dog stops eating for 48 hours, immediately consult a vet or vet tech as this may indicate a serious condition.

A nutritional evaluation by your vet should include assessment of body fat and muscle mass to determine body condition. Monitor your dog's process of eliminating food and water. This may not be as regular as before, but something should happen every day. If that changes, check with your vet or vet tech.

If your dog is not eating well, the first step is to offer new and different foods. Putting some variety into her old menu can go a long way in sparking up her diminished appetite. The focus of eating during palliative care is not so much to maintain a specific body weight or ensure ideal nutrition, but to ensure daily protein intake.

Your dog's meals may become smaller, more frequent and more varied. One type of dog food may work for two or three days, then be ignored. If your dog has primarily eaten dry food in the past, you may renew her interest in eating by switching to canned food, which comes in various flavors and contains water that will help with hydration.

You can rotate canned foods with different flavors every few days to prevent your dog from getting bored or finicky. If this happens, try another, then another, and keep trying until she eats something. Some dogs stop eating because they have lost their sense of smell.

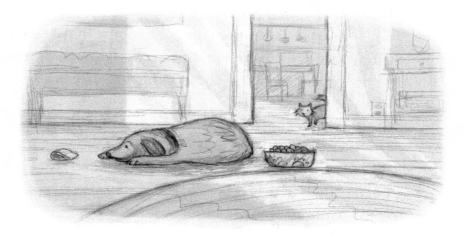

Getting Your Dog to Eat

○ Rotate the type of food: canned vs. dry, new foods and flavors

○ Change the food's temperature. Put canned food in the microwave for 10–15 seconds, using a microwave safe dish, if your dog likes the food warmer. You can also put the food in the freezer for 15 minutes to see if that makes a difference

○ Feed your dog in a different location, even outside

CARING FOR YOUR AGING OR AILING DOG

o   Put the food in a different dish

o   Feed your dog by hand

o   Use flavor enhancers such as maple syrup, brown
    sugar, applesauce, gravy, or fruit yogurt, but keep in
    mind that your dog should not have more than 10%
    of her total daily calories in the form of treats

o   Feed your dog specially prepared dog foods you know
    she likes. Keep trying until it is clear she won't eat
    dog food. Then, you can cook her something that is a
    good source of protein such as:
    •   Ground beef
    •   Ground lamb
    •   Ground chicken
    •   Scrambled eggs

o   Try mixing her foods with other ingredients,
    checking to see which your dog seems to like:
    •   Rice
    •   Grated cheese
    •   Cottage cheese
    •   Mashed potatoes with some butter
    •   Canned pumpkin
    •   Small amounts of peanut butter

When our dog stopped eating, we offered her Italian meatballs that she eagerly devoured for many days (we did, however, hold off on the cannoli). Don't worry about portions; go ahead and let her eat as much as she can. Even if she eats a little, it will help. Despite our success with Italian meatballs, it may not be good to give your dog foods that are high in spices or salt. Spicy food may adversely interact with a sensitive gastrointestinal system and salty food may increase dehydration. That said, we have found that new and interesting foods can make the difference between eating and not eating. When something works, stick with it. If it fails, move on to plan B, C, D, and keep going until you find a new food that clicks.

Unfortunately, your dog cannot complain about how she is feeling. We have found that if a dog is not eating well, she is likely to have some discomfort or indigestion. This can be treated effectively with over-the-counter remedies intended for human consumption – such as Zantac, Pepcid, or Prilosec. Of course, like with any medication, it's always a good idea to check with your vet about dosages. These common OTC medications can be effective in bringing relief to your dog and restoring appetite. A spoonful of Pepto-Bismol in the dinner bowl may also help. None of these will harm your dog.

RESOURCES

Choosing Food for Your Dog

o Burke, A. (2016). Best dog food: Choosing what's right for your dog. *American Kennel Club.* Retrieved from: www.akc.org/content/health/articles/best-dog-food-choosing-whats-right-for-your-dog

o *PetMD. (n.d.) PetMD Nutrition Center.* Retrieved from www.petmd.com/centers/nutrition?icn=TopNav&icl=5_nutrition

o US Food & Drug Administration. (2017, October 13). Pet food labels. *US Food & Drug Administration.* Retrieved from: www.fda.gov/animalveterinary/resourcesforyou/ucm047113.htm

o wikiHow. (n.d.). How to choose healthy dog food. *wikiHow.* Retrieved from: www.wikihow.com/Choose-Healthy-Dog-Food

LUKE

When we adopted him, Luke was a soulful standard English Setter who had been confined to a small cage for more than three years. He was distracted, didn't know his name, his back legs were atrophied, and his hair was yellow from lying in urine. It took about a year to acclimate him to our home and to make real contact with him – but it was worth it. Slowly he started to connect with us. Like a butterfly emerging from its cocoon, his confusion eased and a serene personality, calming energy and unusual elegance emerged. His loving energy was grounding and reassuring. He seemed to be paying us back for rescuing him from a terrible life!

One day I noticed that he was walking awkwardly. I had him evaluated by a neurosurgeon who diagnosed a degenerative spinal disorder. I was devastated, but I tried to focus on the positive: we would still have some years together. I decided to do everything I could to make his life as comfortable and as long as possible. We shared in each other's lives for three more years.

I will admit there were times during Luke's final year when I was unsure if I was doing the right thing. It was heartbreaking to see my brave, loving dog experience difficulty walking, sleeping and eating; incontinence, separation anxiety and increasing dependence. At the same time, with the support of our vet and vet tech, Luke and I were still able to enjoy many wonderful times together.

Our long walks became short walks, and there were times he would trip and fall. When he was no longer able to climb the stairs, I installed a ramp and used a harness with a handle to help this 60 lb. dog upstairs. It was hard to leave him for more than even a few hours because he would fall and become very frightened. To allay his fear as much as possible, I stayed at home as often as I could or had someone stay with him.

We gave Luke pain medication to ensure he was comfortable. When he became incontinent, I bathed him frequently. I shaved his back end, used many "wee-wee pads," washed his beds daily and stayed up with him many nights. I cooked special foods to keep him eating.

It sounds like a lot, doesn't it? The truth is, there were times when it was a struggle. But there were many, many other times when all my efforts felt worth it. He stayed by my side, wagging his tail and grunting with pleasure when I came home. Luke still had a lot of love to give and I tried to give as much as I could in return.

Finally, Luke's ability to walk, roll over – to just be a dog – ebbed away. We knew it was time. We euthanized him at home in familiar surroundings with people who loved him. He remained serene and peaceful until the end – and, in doing so, he gave us all a lesson in unconditional love, grace and dignity in the face of adversity.

–Ellen B.

WALKING

When your dog was young, he was your training partner, accompanying you effortlessly on hikes mile after mile. In the park, he may have marched proudly at your side, head held high, tail waving regally – the envy of every passerby. Now, after running a wild loop around your path, he settles in behind you, just keeping stride. You turn around and realize that he has fallen behind or paused to catch his breath.

LET YOUR DOG SET THE PACE

As your dog gets older, it may be time to let *him* take *you* for a walk. Let him set the pace. The walk may be slower paced and shorter, but this will give you more time to smell the roses. Your dog will get the same pleasure and stimulation from his outing as before and you may learn to see, hear and even smell as well as he does.

Whatever the pace or duration, *it is important to continue to walk with your dog* as part of a daily routine. He will let you know his limits.

While on an outing, many older dogs still love to play fetch, carry, and other games that give them exercise. Sometimes they will let you know when they have had enough, even if it is after only one toss of the ball. That's okay! He is still enjoying himself and moving about. Some older dogs are able to swim. Good! Dive in with your dog – swimming is a low impact activity that is very beneficial for both the four and the two legged.

Walking outdoors in winter conditions can become a challenge for an older dog. If walking in snow is more difficult for your dog, you should shovel a path. If you use an "ice melt" product, make sure it is safe for animals. Also, you may want to try some winter gear for your dog: The Ruffwear Company offers non-skid booties that work well in normal winter conditions.

KEEP YOUR DOG WALKING

- o Keep your dog active

- o Provide nutritious food and hydration

- o Maintain average weight

- o Create a routine that meets his changing needs

- o Cover wooden and tile floors

- o Create a safe, confined space in your home

- o Use a harness, *Bottom's Up Leash*, or bath towel

- o Use ramps between rooms for short stairs

- o Use non-skid booties or shovel a path in ice and snow

- o If necessary, provide pain relief with medication, physical therapy, heating pad and acupuncture

NAVIGATING STAIRS

Dogs love their routines. If your dog sleeps upstairs in your bedroom at night, an inability to go upstairs can feel like a real hardship. A dog who has difficulty with stairs may have to live on the ground floor. You can create a comfortable space for him with his bed and other belongings and stay with him before he falls asleep. You may need to install a safety gate to prevent your dog from trying to navigate the stairs.

Various aids can help dogs who have difficulty walking. Small dogs can be easily carried, but ambulatory problems can be very difficult for large dogs. When one of our dogs had increasing difficulty with walking, we used a Ruffwear Harness. By using the handle on the body harness, we could ensure that he didn't fall when we walked him. We could help him go upstairs, get him up from lying on the floor, and assist him walking on wood and tile floors without slipping. The harness is easy to put on, can be washed, and our dog seemed to find it comfortable. Moving him from room to room was like carrying a 60-pound suitcase but using this harness may have significantly prolonged his life as he became weaker, so the heavy lifting was worth it.

Another option is using the Bottom's Up Leash in lieu of a bulkier harness. This supports the hind legs of a dog whose legs are weak and doesn't interfere with peeing and pooping. The leash can be easily washed with soap and water.

You can also improvise with a large bath towel used as a sling by placing it underneath the dog's midsection. This will allow you to help your dog walk around and provide the additional support necessary to help him go up and down stairs. A little strategic thinking is in order: make sure that you place the towel in a way that doesn't interfere with your dog's urination – we learned that one the hard way!

You can also use a small ramp similar in design to a wheelchair ramp to help your dog negotiate short flights of stairs into your house, or between rooms indoors on the same floor. Slowly acclimate your dog to the ramp because some dogs will be frightened by the new terrain and will need to be taught how to use it. You can provide support while your dog goes up and down a few times. Entice him by holding a treat in front of him. After a few practice runs, he will be able to use the ramp with no problem.

For small or medium dogs, you can buy small portable stairs at a pet store to help your dog get on and off the beds and couches. Or go the do-it-yourself route and make your own by using a stack of throw pillows or an ottoman.

WOOD AND TILE FLOORS

As walking problems progress, navigating slippery wood or tile floors can become challenging. Luckily, this is an easy fix. Start by covering wooden and tile floors with yoga mats, rubber mats, runners with non-skid surfaces, or carpets. You can also place small plastic rings on your dog's toes to provide extra traction (see "Resources" at end of this chapter).

Regular dog manicures are another easy fix: keeping your dog's nails trimmed will decrease the possibility of slipping on wood and tile floors. When you are not home and your dog is alone you can also restrict your dog to safer, contained areas of the house, or even in a crate. If you've never used a dog crate, it might feel a little strange at first, but mostly for you. Dogs enjoy the secure feeling of resting in a doggie crate. Think of it as an extra secure dog house.

CONSIDER A PROFESSIONAL EVALUATION

When you notice that your dog's pace starts to slow and he tires before you do, it is time to have her checked by a veterinarian. Is she developing an issue with her heart that could be made worse by vigorous exercise? Is she becoming arthritic and would benefit from anti-inflammatory medication?

If your dog has been a healthy weight most or all her life, arthritis will most likely appear later than if she has been overweight for years. Regardless, shedding any extra pounds now can improve her function dramatically. During evaluation, your veterinarian may suggest thyroid testing since hypothyroidism is a common hormonal abnormality in dogs. Correcting a low thyroid level may help your dog lose weight and feel younger.

Arthritis in dogs is a painful condition for which many medications and treatments are available. The mainstay of arthritis treatment is using non-steroidal anti-inflammatory drugs (NSAIDS). These are canine equivalents of Advil or Aleve for humans (see chapter on Pain). However, do *not use over-the-counter human NSAIDS for any canine*. NSAIDS approved for dogs – carprofen, meloxicam and others – are available only by prescription. They all contain a warning to discontinue use if a dog experiences loss of appetite, vomiting, or diarrhea. Dogs' stomachs are extremely sensitive to the ulcer-causing effects of these drugs. When prescribed, these medications should always be given with food to protect your dog's stomach.

Other medications can be used if your dog cannot tolerate NSAIDS or you need to increase the effects to provide your dog more pain control. Many dogs benefit from non-prescription dietary supplements including glucosamine, chondroitin, Omega 3 fatty acids, and anti-oxidants. Regular acupuncture treatment can also be effective.

A dog with chronic hind end weakness or hind end pain will usually develop big, beefy shoulders from over-compensating by pulling his body forward with his front legs rather than pushing from behind. There will be a corresponding atrophy of the muscles of the hips and back legs, giving the dog a triangular profile when viewed from above. Your veterinarian will palpate your dog's back and legs carefully, moving each joint front, back and to the sides. Radiographs will most likely be suggested.

Your veterinarian will also check out your dog's neurological status. A common test is performed by rolling the dog's feet under one at a time to see if the dog returns the foot to a normal position before placing it back on the floor. If a dog fails to do this, it suggests a neurological deficit, such as a loss of "conscious proprioception," the non-visual sense of where one's body is in space. This may also indicate "degenerative myelopathy" related to degeneration of the long nerves that run from the spinal cord to the rear end of the body and hind legs. Although not painful, it is progressive and has no definitive treatment.

PHYSICAL REHABILITATION

Animal physical rehabilitation centers – equipped with underwater treadmills and exercise swimming pools – are now available in some communities. These centers offer different therapies such as laser, ultrasound and shock wave therapy. A rehabilitation specialist can train dog owners in therapeutic massage, gentle stretching and specific exercises for the dog to improve strength, flexibility, range of motion and agility.

We took our aging English Setter to a rehabilitation facility where he swam in a pool and walked on a treadmill while in the water. They then set up a small obstacle course for him to walk around to increase his strength and agility. They also suggested various exercises we could do together at home. The canine rehab facility gave our dog benefits well worth the cost and time. Just like with his owners, it turned out going to the gym worked wonders even though they don't have a doggie steam room – at least not yet.

RESOURCES

- American Veterinary Medical Association. (n.d.). *Disease precautions for dog walkers.* American Veterinary Medical Association. Retrieved from: www.avma.org/KB/Resources/Pages/disease-precautions-dog-walkers.aspx

- American Veterinary Medical Association. (n.d.). *Walking with your pet.* American Veterinary Medical Association. Retrieved from: www.avma.org/public/PetCare/Pages/Walking-with-Your-Pet.aspx

- Andrews, L.W. (2014). Dog walking has psychological benefits for you. *Psychology Today.* Retrieved from: www.psychologytoday.com/blog/minding-the-body/201404/dog-walking-has-psychological-benefits-you

Gear: Walking Your Dog

- Bottom's Up Leash. www.bottomsupleash.com

- Runners, rugs, and mats with non-skid backing. Available at: www.consolidatedplastics.com

- Doggon Wheelchair available at: www.doggon.com

- Eddie's Wheels for Pets available at: www.eddieswheels.com

- Dr. Buzby's ToeGrips for Dogs available at: www.toegrips.com

- Products for handicapped pets available at: www.handicappedpets.com

- Help 'Em Up Harness available at: www.helpemup.com

- Ruffwear Harness available at: www.ruffwear.com

- Ruffwear Non-skid Booties available at: www.ruffwear.com

VIVIAN

Vivian was our greyhound, a retired racing dog who washed out at the track. We adopted her from a shelter that specializes in saving greyhounds once their racing days are over. Many greyhounds are abandoned and abused. On her first night with us in her new home, we spent an hour removing ticks from her belly.

Vivian was strong and regal, and even though she no longer raced competitively, she could still run faster that any dog we had ever seen. When we moved from the city to the country, she loved the open spaces. We marveled at her ability to speed over rough terrain without missing a step.

One Thanksgiving Day, while visiting family and walking in a city park, we let Vivian off her leash. She ran off in a wide circle, then suddenly yelped, and fell to the ground. We carried her home, fearing her right front leg was fractured or broken. An X-ray revealed far worse: she had bone cancer. We were told it would progress and develop rapidly.

We considered amputation which can work well for many dogs with bone cancer in a leg. A greyhound, however, is a special breed. One of the fastest animals on earth, greyhounds are hobbled more than other dogs with only three legs. Instead, we built a handicap ramp at our back door to help her get in and out of the house.

We were determined to continue caring for Vivian as long as her circumstances were tolerable, but as the cancer progressed, we soon knew that Vivian was headed toward the end of her life.

We felt we would know – and she would let us know – when the time had come. And she did.

Vivian had many fine days in the last weeks of her life. We were happy to give those to her – and to have them for us. And we are ready to adopt another dog from the recue shelter again.

–John K.

HYGIENE

Ensuring good hygiene and general cleanliness includes protection of your dog's skin from infection and attention to dental care. Good hygiene is extremely important in supporting your aging or ailing dog.

A significant part of care for an ailing dog is managing challenges with eating, digesting, peeing and pooping. Various bodily functions that once were fairly straightforward may now present a health hazard. Hygiene is extremely important to increase your dog's comfort, and minimize health hazards to your dog, and to you as well.

It can be frustrating for you and your pet when she can't get up in time to go outside to do her "business" without your assistance. Some dogs may be unable to support themselves long enough to pee or poop without help (see Walking chapter for tips on helping your dog to walk and be more mobile). Or your dog may be unaware that she needs to urinate or defecate. She may just feel stressed and bark excessively when she realizes that she can't get up and out in time (see Incontinence chapter).

KEEPING YOUR DOG CLEAN AND DRY

It is imperative that you keep your dog's skin clean and dry. If her skin is always wet from urine or stools that becomes caked, she is at risk for infection, skin rashes, and bed sores. Not to mention that it doesn't leave her feeling or smelling fresh. If your dog's skin becomes infected and breaks down, this can become life-threatening, especially for aging and ailing dogs.

A trip to the spa could be in order to protect your dog from infections. A nice, very short "puppy cut" all over her body can go a long way towards keeping her skin clean and manageable. Trim her hair very short and keep her belly and groin areas shaved to help keep these areas clean. Long-haired dogs, especially those with feathers at their back end and tail, are at higher risk of developing skin infections. If it isn't too stressful for your dog, shave her down to help keep maintenance at a minimum. You might not be able to teach an old dog new tricks, but you can always give an old dog a new hairstyle.

Dogs in danger of skin infection may need baths more frequently than younger dogs. Use a shampoo specifically designated for dogs, since human skin is more acidic and human shampoos can interfere with a dog's acidic mantle. Do not use shampoo that contains zinc pyrithione. Make sure your dog is rinsed thoroughly and completely dried after each bath, especially in colder months. Baby powder and zinc-free skin creams can help protect your dog's skin in sensitive areas. Just like with humans, your dog will feel fresher, peppier, and healthier if you follow these three simple rules: lather, rinse, repeat!

Daily bathing may become a part of your dog's routine at this stage of her life. With small dogs, this is much easier. As anyone who has ever tried to bathe a big dog knows – it's a sloppy affair! As they get older too it may get harder to get your big dog in and out of the tub. What was once a one-man job might now be a two-man job, so plan ahead: invite a friend over for a dog-bathing party. In nice weather, for those of you in the suburbs, this can be an outdoor party! Fire up the grill in the backyard, invite a friend over and give that pup a scrub.

DENTAL PROBLEMS CAN BECOME HEALTH PROBLEMS

Keeping your dog's teeth clean is an important preventive strategy from the time your dog is young. Dental care becomes even more important for an aging or ailing dog. Dental disease may be the most common problem that vets see in dogs.

If you brush your dog's teeth regularly, you will decrease the likelihood of infections, gum disease and tooth decay. Without frequent brushing, many dogs develop dental problems, even at a young age. Older dogs often have dental disease that may affect their ability to eat and may lead to more serious health issues. Many old dogs accumulate calculus and plaques, and can develop gum disease (gingivitis), ulcerative lesions and tooth loss.

The ideal dental routine includes daily teeth brushing, dental checkups and professional cleaning when necessary. Many dog treats on the market claim to reduce dental disease, but regular brushing is the best approach. According to Dr. William Rosenblad, DVM, of Angell Memorial Medical Center, "the bristles are able to get below the gum line and are best at removing plaque." Plaque is the material that often turns into tartar which contributes to gum recession, bone loss, and eventual loss of teeth.

For older dogs who have not had a regular dental routine, consider beginning one. Start slowly – a few teeth at a time. Approach the dog from the side, hold her still, and brush a few teeth at a time with a soft-to-medium bristled brush. Focus on the outside surfaces of the teeth and be sure to brush her back teeth. It is important to get to the gum/tooth line where disease occurs. You can use toothpaste, but it isn't essential. If you choose a toothpaste, pick one that contains an enzymatic cleanser; these products contain an ingredient "ase" (e.g., lactoperoxidase).

If your dog doesn't tolerate a toothbrush, try using a rubber thimble or gauze that you wrap around your finger. If your dog is resistant, try coupling brushing with a treat to reinforce the experience and make it as positive a process as you can.

Older dogs with dental problems may need a professional cleaning, that requires anesthesia. The cleaning should be followed up with regular brushing at home – not very different from how humans maintain their oral hygiene, except we don't need anesthesia because we can (usually) stay still in the dental chair. Be sure to talk to your vet about dental health and the risk of using general anesthesia in a senior dog.

Your older dog is probably not ever going to have a perfect, movie-star white Tom Cruise smile, but with a little extra attention to oral hygiene, she won't have to put her teeth in a glass at night.

Brushing Your Dog's Teeth

○ Brush your dog's teeth daily or as often as you can.

○ Use a soft to medium texture nylon-filament brush.

o Finger brush or use soft gauze if your dog won't accept the toothbrush.

o Use only toothpaste designated for dogs.

o Use tasty toothpaste, especially with a resistant dog.

o Begin with a few teeth at a time until the dog gets used to brushing. You can straddle the dog from behind and begin brushing his back teeth—moving forward with circular motions.

o Focus on the outside (buccal) parts of the teeth. Be sure to also brush the gums.

o Reward your dog at the end of the brushing session.

Caring for Your Dog's Oral Hygiene

o Give your dog food that encourages chewing since this increases saliva flow.

o Ask your vet to check your dog's teeth periodically.

o Discuss chemical plaque retardants with your vet. These are designed for dogs that won't accept brushing and have serious gum disease.

○ Check with your vet about whether professional cleaning may be necessary.

SKIN PROBLEMS

As a dog ages, her muzzle may become grey or white. Her skin may thicken and become less pliable. Some dogs will have areas of hair loss and many develop calluses over pressure points, such as the elbows.

Older dogs are more likely to develop skin growths, including lipomas – benign fat bubbles under the skin that can often be seen or felt. Lipomas can become very large. These do not require immediate treatment, but should be monitored for sudden growth, oozing and bleeding. Lipomas can sometimes become liposarcomas (malignant tumors) and require medical attention. Some dog owners prefer to have lipomas surgically removed before they become problematic.

Grooming can help to prevent skin problems and ensure good hygiene. If you are going to groom your dog yourself, extra caution is advisable. Most importantly, clippers should be used rather than scissors to prevent the possibility of cutting the dog's skin when removing matted fur especially behind the ears, around the butt and around the tail.

Remember when you trimmed your dog's nails to help her keep from slipping on hard floors? This also helps prevent health problems that occur from the splintering or breaking of a toenail. If you groom your dog's nails yourself, be aware of the quick in the dog's nail, which is a blood vessel. Most pet clinics will provide a demonstration of how best to trim nails.

Battery operated nail filers are available and easy to use. At first, use it on the slowest speed to introduce your dog to the sensation and noise of the tool.

Beauty is not just skin deep – your dog is beautiful all the way through. However, skin problems are skin deep, so keep your dog's surface beautiful AND healthy with a good skin-care regimen.

RESOURCES

Gear: Bath Time

o *Pro Guard Dog Grooming Stay-N-Wash Tub Restraint.* Available at: <u>www.petedge.com</u>

- *Rinse Ace Bathing Tethers.* Available at: www.rinseace.com

Gear: Dental Care

- Chewy Dog Dental Care. Available at: www.chewy.com

- Petrodex Enzymatic Toothpaste. Available at: www.amazon.com

- Vibrac Control Enzymatic Toothpaste. Available at: www.amazon.com

- KissAble Dog Toothpaste. Available at: www.amazon.com

Gear: Grooming

- Groomer's Choice Grooming Tools. Available at: www.groomerschoice.com

- Dremel Pet Grooming Kit. Available at: www.dremel.com

INCONTINENCE

Incontinence is one of the most difficult symptoms of old age and illness for a dog owner to manage. Incontinence can ruin your carpets, dog beds and even your hardwood floors. It is hard to clean up and hard on your house. You may find that you are running your washing machine every day to keep up.

It's stressful – for you and your dog. There is a natural human reaction to bodily waste in the wrong place – we don't like it! Your dog knows this, too. He's not happy about it either.

It's important to accept the fact that at this stage of life, your dog is going to need a little extra help in this department.

A few simple adjustments can greatly reduce the stress for both owner and dog – and have a positive impact on your dog's physical well-being.

Above all, it is necessary to keep your dog clean and dry, so his skin will not break down and become infected.

URINARY INCONTINENCE

As dogs get older, many develop varying degrees of urinary incontinence. Some dribble urine where they are lying down or while they sleep. Others lose full control of their bladder function.

Aging results in decreased bladder capacity and urethral tone that may lead to a lessened ability to retain urine. However, before you assume that the incontinence is due to old age, have your vet evaluate your dog for chronic renal failure, urinary tract infections and other causes such as tumors. Loss of urine should be discussed with your vet.

Sometimes, a problem is behavioral. Whatever the cause, remember that your dog can't help it. Incontinence should always be viewed as a medical problem that needs to be diagnosed and managed. Never punish your dog for incontinence. This is counterproductive.

Incontinence is far more likely to develop in elderly spayed female dogs. Overall, almost 20% of female dogs – especially large breeds – are likely to develop some form of incontinence as they age. The most common cause is urethral incompetence that develops as dogs get older and most often manifests when the dog is asleep or relaxing. Urinary incontinence in males may be the result of a prostate problem, but this is relatively uncommon.

What You Can Do About Urinary Incontinence

o Always maintain a calm and supportive approach with your dog. Never punish him for incontinence.

o Ask your vet to evaluate the incontinence and identify medical approaches to treat it.

o Consult with your vet about the safety of limiting your dog's water intake.

o Be vigilant about the possibility of a developing infection. Urine can become smelly, and skin can become red and begin to break down.

o Establish a schedule of frequent, timed walks. Walk your dog more frequently especially when he finishes eating, first gets up from a nap or after playing.

o Cover his dog bed with towels that you can easily wash and put a plastic sheet under the towels.

o Use various pads to absorb the urine.

o Get leak-proof pads at your pet store that come in different sizes. Put them where the dog sleeps or lies down. Be sure to change them when they are damp or wet. (See section on Fecal Incontinence below.)

o Use an absorbent sanitary napkin and put it in place with a snug Velcro fastening kit around your dog's back.

o Use doggie diapers, available at many pet stores. Be sure you change them frequently to ensure the dog's skin remains dry. Your dog should never lay around in a soiled diaper, or there is risk of skin break down and infection. Also, be aware: your dog might try to eat a wet diaper and that's a mess no one wants.

o For smaller dogs, consider using a litter box that can be filled with cat litter, artificial turf or lined with paper, and teach your dog to use it. For large dogs, buy a square tray designed to catch leaks under a refrigerator or washing machine and place a leak-proof pad in it.

o Keep your dog dry around the genitalia by carefully shaving the hair in the private area. You can ask your vet tech to do this periodically. After urination or leaking, clean the area with a damp towel and then dry with a dry towel.

o Give your dog more frequent baths if the urine leaks onto the body and legs.

o   If your dog sleeps on your bed, you may have to change
      this behavior. You can acclimate him to sleeping in a bed
      on the floor or confine him at night in a crate or a
      smaller space.

o   Check under the dog's bed to make sure the urine hasn't
      leaked onto your floor. Make sure the bed is dry through
      and through. Even if the top of the bed is dry, the urine
      can leak through. Wash the bed often.

o   Use shower curtain liners or a sheet of plastic under the
      bedding to protect the floor.

o   If necessary, provide an indoor place near his bed for
      your dog to urinate, and teach him to go there.

FECAL INCONTINENCE

Fecal incontinence, or the inability to control bowel
movements, is often a turning point in an owner's decision
about when to end palliative care. The natural human disgust
with feces can make it very difficult for those that feel
incontinence is too offensive to try to manage.

For some people, these feelings are too hard to overcome.
Other owners find ways to manage this problem, so their dog
can live longer with dignity.

Many old dogs have severe pain when defecating because of
arthritis in their back, neurological impairments or anal
sphincter problems that interfere with the cues that suggest

they need to go outside to poop. One old dog we cared for developed increasing weakness in his back end and atrophy of all his muscles there. Eventually, he could no longer arch his back to poop and to walk.

It is not uncommon for elderly dogs to fall and then defecate, especially when their owner has gone out for a while. As our old dog became increasingly hobbled and unsteady, we would try not to leave him for many hours. Sometimes this couldn't be avoided, and we would come home to find him panicked, unable to get up and lying in his feces.

After trying to calm him down and comfort him, we would bathe him and clean up the floor. It was exhausting for us and our dog.

What You Can Do to Reduce Fecal Incontinence

○   Change your pet's diet to increase the likelihood that the stool will be more solid. Use of dry rather than canned food may help.

○   Add high fiber supplements such as Metamucil or add high fiber foods to his diet such as a scoop of canned pumpkin (or other orange vegetable), bran cereal or sweet potatoes.

○   Some vets suggest that a diet low in fiber will produce smaller solid stools. To do this, you can feed your dog cottage cheese, rice or tofu.

- o Feed your dog on a fixed schedule, perhaps twice a day with a snack in between. Sometimes this will increase the likelihood of pooping predictably after a meal.

- o Use frequent warm water enemas to decrease the volume of feces and inappropriate defecation.

- o Apply a warm washcloth or pinch the rear end of your dog to induce defecation.

- o Consider pain medications. If the major cause of your dog's incontinence is discomfort about arching his back to poop, then talk with your vet about trying various pain medications. Adding acupuncture as well as comprehensive treatment for arthritis may also help relieve pain.

- o Walk your dog frequently, and after meals and naps.

- o Confine the dog to a separate room (e.g., kitchen) or put him in his crate if you leave.

- o Clean any place where the dog has soiled to eliminate any residual odors that may prompt him to do this again at the same spot.

Strategies to Manage Ongoing Fecal Incontinence

o   Allow your dog to poop wherever she is, then clean up the area and the dog.

o   If your dog defecates in the house, clean up the stool and vigorously wash the area with soap and water, and spray it with Nature's Miracle, an organic cleaner. Make sure your dog is clean; this may require washing and drying his rear end to ensure his skin will not break down.

o   Shave your dog's back end so that cleaning your dog is easier.

o   If your dog defecates after meals or at a somewhat regular time, confine him temporarily to a section of the house with a bare floor or tile to make cleaning up easier.

o   Express your dog's bowel. This approach is not for the squeamish. You can stimulate your dog to poop using methods such as: (a) chlorhexidine with water sprayed into his anus; (b) ice rubbed around his anal sphincter; (c) squirting water in the anal area at specified times – often twice a day; and (d) stimulating his anus with your gloved finger. For various strategies go to:
www.handicappedpets.com

Gear: Incontinence

- Only Natural Pet Incontinence Remedies. Available at www.onlynaturalpet.com

- Chewy Potty Pads. Available at www.chewy.com

SHOWBOY

For the last year of his life, our adopted Collie had severe arthritis in his hips. He was unable to get up from a lying position on his own, so we would help lift his hips until he was able to stand. Once up, Showboy was unsteady on his feet, sometimes falling down. The first stair step in our house − between the great room and the kitchen − was particularly challenging.

Showboy was taking pain medication (tramadol) and daily dietary supplements (omega-3 fatty acids, glucosamine and chondroitin) prescribed to ease pain and stiffness from arthritis. Since he could not stand up on his own to get a drink of water, or even shift to a more comfortable position, we adjusted our routine so we were never away from home for longer than three hours.

Watching this gorgeous, robust champion lose his independence was heartbreaking. It was hard to accept that all the love in the world could not save him. As his disease progressed, Showboy was unable to relieve himself properly, or lie down with any comfort. His discomfort grew so great, it didn't seem right to make him suffer these indignities. After a long, sleepless night of him pacing and unable to rest, we decided to end his pain and suffering.

It is said that dogs love unconditionally and Showboy's sweet, gentle nature never wavered. Looking back, I know we only had one concern: doing what was best for Showboy. I am surprised that I could care for another being tirelessly without complaint or resentment. I am grateful for the joy and grace he brought into our lives. We learn so much from our dogs – not only how to live but how to die.

–Brenda P.

VOMITING AND DIARRHEA

As your dog ages or deals with illness, her system may become increasingly vulnerable to vomiting or diarrhea. This is very likely to occur in your house (and on your rugs and carpets) rather than more conveniently in the yard or on the sidewalk.

When vomiting or diarrhea goes on for days or even weeks, it tries the patience of any caretaker. These symptoms may be commonplace occurrences in end-of-life circumstances and may continue until it's over. For some dog owners, this can be a deal breaker. You should understand your capacity to be regularly confronted with cleaning up your house and your dog, but you should give yourself a chance to accommodate to his needs.

REGURGITATING AND VOMITING

Occasional regurgitation and vomiting is common in all dogs. Regurgitation usually involves materials from a dog's mouth and esophagus, or from foods that have not been fully absorbed in his stomach.

If your dog regurgitates, check for some of the usual offenders: grass or plants from your garden, animal matter, or unusual foods that he is not used to eating. If your dog looks and acts fine after an episode of this kind, then you don't need to do anything further. However, if the regurgitation continues, check your dog's mouth to be sure he hasn't ingested any objects and that there are no signs of obvious trauma to his mouth.

You also might check for enlarged lymph nodes on either side of his Adam's apple. If these are enlarged or tender, be sure to consult your vet. If your dog also has diarrhea, or a painful or distended abdomen, be sure to call your vet or bring your dog to an animal hospital immediately to rule out an obstruction or other serious causes.

Episodes of vomiting often begin with your dog behaving differently or seeming uncomfortable. He may shiver, yawn, lick his lips, hide, or begin retching. Then he will throw up his gastric contents. Usually, the dog will recover quickly. However, if the vomiting doesn't stop within 1 to 2 days or intensifies, contact your vet. During that period, you can feed your dog cottage cheese and boiled skinless chicken and rice to settle his system. You can also use antacids with guidance from your vet.

Most of the time, vomiting is not a cause for alarm. Bring your dog to the vet if it continues, your dog seems dehydrated, has little energy, has a fever or is in pain. If the expelled materials are black, bloody or look like coffee grinds, bring your dog to the vet immediately.

What You Can Do About Vomiting

o   After vomiting stops, do not give your dog water or feed him for 8 to 12 hours and limit his activity.

o   After this period, offer the dog small amounts of water or crushed ice. If he manages this easily, feed him with readily digestible food. This can include small, frequent feedings of cottage cheese or skinless chicken and rice.

o   If your dog is refusing water, offer him ¼ to 1/3 cup of low sodium chicken broth or beef broth added to water for no more than one to two days.

o   During this period, if your dog is usually fed twice a day, divide these portions into four feedings per day.

o   If vomiting stops, return your dog to a normal diet within two to four days.

o Be cautious about feeding your dog table scraps or allowing him to get into the garbage.

o Antacids, e.g. famotidine (Pepcid) or Prilosec, can help reduce symptoms of gastric reflux, gastritis and ulcers from illnesses like colitis or pancreatitis.

o Talk to your vet about using Gastorfate or other stomach protectants to help protect your dog's stomach from ulcers if he is on other medications or NSAIDS, or is nauseated or vomiting.

o After discussion with your vet, consider using anti-emetics like Cerenia. For example, dogs with chronic renal disease are often nauseated and will benefit from this medication.

DIARRHEA

Most dogs experience brief episodes of diarrhea. If your dog has a few bouts of diarrhea over a short period, these may resolve on their own.

The two most common causes of diarrhea are a dietary indiscretion or an obstruction. If your dog has a history of eating things she shouldn't, or she has gotten into the trash and may have eaten a bone, you should contact your vet. Your dog may need an X-ray. Diarrhea may also be caused by intestinal parasites. It's a good idea to bring a stool sample to your vet for testing to rule this out.

What You Can Do About Diarrhea

o For a brief episode of diarrhea, withhold your dog's regular food for 24 hours or feed your dog rice water during this period. To make rice water, boil one cup of white rice in 4 cups of water; let the water cool before giving it to your dog. Do not use minute rice or brown rice, which has too much fiber.

o Then move to small servings of solid food, including boiled white rice or pasta, which both provide starch. You can also boil chicken, ground turkey, or low-fat hamburger to provide adequate protein. Always boil meat rather than frying it. Cottage cheese is a good source of protein that doesn't require any cooking.

o Once the diarrhea stops for at least 24 hours, start your dog back on his regular food using a bland diet. These foods are available at your local vet or animal hospital, or your vet may suggest some commercially available bland diet options such as:
  - Hills I/d and w/d, available in wet and dry formulas
  - Purina EN Naturals, wet and dry formulas
  - Purina DCO, dry only
  - Royal Canine Gastrointestinal Low Fat, wet and dry formula

You can reintroduce your dog's regular diet by using ¾ bland diet to ¼ original diet for 4 to 5 days, then ½ bland ½ original for 4 to 5 days, then ¼ bland to ¾ original for 4 to 5 days. If at any time during this transition, diarrhea or loose stools return, go back to the 100% bland diet and feed it to your dog for a longer period. It can take a few weeks or longer to transition your dog back to regular food. Be patient.

Old or ailing dogs may become increasingly sensitive to various foods. Even if your dog has eaten the same food for years, he can suddenly develop a food allergy or intolerance that can cause diarrhea. It may be necessary to switch your dog to a permanent bland diet to prevent diarrhea from recurring.

With an old or ailing dog, diarrhea can rapidly lead to dehydration, so the dog should be carefully monitored. If a dog becomes dehydrated, he may require subcutaneous or even intravenous fluids; this should be determined by your vet. Your vet may treat your dog's diarrhea using metronidazole (Flagyl), Panacur or other oral de-wormers.

During a period of diarrhea, contact your vet if you see the following symptoms in your dog:

o   Not drinking water
o   Signs of dehydration
o   Diarrhea continues for longer than 24 hours

REX

Our adopted Shetland Sheepdog Rex began to have digestive issues. He couldn't finish his meals and had periodic, unexplained bouts of nausea for weeks. Our vet completed a blood panel and diagnosed Rex as anemic.

As we began to rule out and treat different potential causes for the anemia, his symptoms worsened. An ultrasound indicated a mass in his intestine and we were referred to an oncologist for further treatment. After emergency surgery to remove and test the mass, a new diagnosis arrived — Rex had cancer. After consulting with our oncologist to consider treatment, prognosis and cost, we opted to move forward with chemotherapy.

Rex tolerated his intravenous chemotherapy well during the first couple of sessions. But after a few weeks, we noticed a knot on his neck. A biopsy revealed that he had a Mast Cell Grade 3 tumor. Rex underwent surgery again and the oncologist recommended additional chemotherapy.

This second diagnosis forced us to think through a chemotherapy plan to address two separate, but deadly forms of cancer. This was uncharted territory for our oncologist, and we weighed the pros and cons of stopping treatment, treating just one cancer, or attempting to treat both. We decided to alternate two chemotherapy regimens every 6 weeks. Rex responded extremely well, showing no return of the cancer and few physical side effects, with only a slight upset stomach on the day of the chemotherapy sessions.

Unfortunately, our ultimate decision to let Rex go was not based on his cancer, but spinal stenosis. It occurred suddenly and caused him extreme pain. He was unable to stand or be touched without triggering howling pain. It is possible the chemotherapy contributed to degeneration of his vertebra, but we ultimately felt that we made the right decision to continue treatment after his initial cancer diagnoses. Chemotherapy gave him a good quality of life for almost a year before the intolerable and intractable pain from the spinal stenosis set in.

Making treatment decisions about the medical care of your dog is personal. For Rex, we had to consider his ability to undergo treatment, the financial implications and the emotional impact of our decisions. The process required educating ourselves, communicating closely with veterinary surgeons and oncologists, and coordinating care with our regular vet and specialists. Although we still miss him, we feel that we made the right decisions for Rex and for us.

—Kathleen F.

PAIN

Incredibly, it was once an accepted fact that dogs do not feel pain. Of course, we now know better. Pain management is a central feature of palliative and hospice care. As we learn more about dogs and are better able to manage their pain, many people are choosing to give their dogs as much time as is manageable and comfortable, regardless of the difficulties this may present.

All dogs, like people, occasionally experience pain and sometimes experience it chronically. Unlike people, dogs cannot describe their pain. Most dogs are stoic by nature: in the wild an injured or sick dog is a liability to the whole pack and is likely to be shunned.

Old age in dogs increases the likelihood of periods of sustained pain. For example, osteoarthritis in one or more joints occurs in approximately 80 percent of dogs older than 8 years. In addition to chronic pain, an acute condition such as cancer may cause a new level of pain, signaling a potentially serious or life-threatening condition. Managing pain in our canine friends is vital to providing humane care.

We – as our dog's family – are in the best position to observe subtle signs of discomfort. We observe our dogs throughout the day and can notice the general location and relative intensity of our pet's discomfort. When pain begins to trouble an older dog, it is best to consult a veterinarian.

Good pain management is complex. Since our dogs cannot describe their pain, we must speak for them. Identifying and addressing painful conditions early, such as joint disease in its early stages, can give our pets many more years of active and fun life.

There are better ways to treat pain than immediately resorting to euthanasia. But, first, you have to be able to identify it.

SIGNS OF DISCOMFORT AND PAIN

Your dog may show discomfort in a variety of ways. She may develop new behaviors such as preferring to stay outdoors by herself in the cold. One of our golden retrievers dug a hole in the backyard during the winter and burrowed herself in, something she had never done before. We found out that she was gravely ill, and she died soon afterwards.

You may notice restlessness, especially in the evening and night, in the form of pacing, a sigh, a moan or a soft whimpering. Knowing your dog well, you may notice changes in her posture or facial expression. Signs of pain to watch for include verbal cues, behavioral differences, and visible discomfort.

Verbal Cues

o Whining or whimpering
o Howling or yelping
o Growling

Facial Cues

o Dull expression
o Glazed eyes
o Squinting
o Grimacing
o Ears flat or pinned

Change in Posture

o Head hanging low (often the sign of neck pain)
o Arched back and/or tucked belly (frequently a sign of abdominal pain)
o Sitting hunched

o   Lying in odd positions or not stretching out on his side

Change in Habits

o   Depressed appetite
o   Increased or decreased water consumption
o   Decreased stamina
o   Difficulty getting up or down
o   Slow, stilted gait
o   Difficulty bearing weight
o   Decreased grooming
o   Licking or biting body parts (e.g., licking arthritic joints)
o   Incontinence or the loss of house training
o   Nighttime restlessness

Change in Behavior

o   Withdrawing or hiding
o   Lack of interest in surroundings
o   Avoiding human interaction and touch or being overly clingy and needy
o   Agitation/ restlessness
o   Depression
o   Irritability

You may find that touching a painful area on your dog may elicit a cry or a growl. He may even nip at your hand. Don't scold your dog; try to be sympathetic. Respect this warning and avoid touching the painful area.

Two of our golden retrievers developed metastatic cancer, but we did not know it until a week before each of them died. They were both 12 years old. Rusty, a loving deep red golden retriever, seemed her usual self until she went out into the backyard one afternoon, dug a deep hole and crawled in. She refused to come out until we coaxed her with treats. We immediately brought her to the vet. She was evaluated and operated on for a hemangiosarcoma (a rapidly growing cancer particular to dogs) of her heart. Sadly, Rusty died a week later. Golden retrievers have a higher rate of cancer compared to other breeds. They commonly develop lymphomas or hemangiosarcomas.

Max was an almost white, moderately sized golden retriever who was a calm, loving and empathic companion. One day on a routine walk, he collapsed. We rushed him to the vet and he was diagnosed with a large bleeding tumor in his abdomen, probably a hemangiosarcoma. Over the next four days, with the help of pain meds, we attempted to stabilize him. We stayed with Max until the end, cuddling and sleeping together on the floor of the living room.

Both dogs must have been in considerable discomfort during the weeks leading up to their sudden deaths. Neither gave any indication that they were suffering. Dogs have an impressive capacity to shoulder pain. By the time they are actually complaining, they may have been feeling pain for some time.

PROVIDING COMFORT

As your dog begins to age, talk with your veterinarian or vet tech about what you can do now to make the future better for your senior dog. Decide whether your vet visits should be increased.

How to Support Your Aging or Ailing Dog

o Help your dog get to and maintain a healthy weight.

o Continue exercise within your dog's comfort zone.

o Have dental care done if needed. A diseased mouth causes pain and spreads bacteria throughout a dog's body.

o Use heat or ice when beneficial.

o Make accommodations in your house:
   - A thick soft bed for sleep.
   - Non-slip surfaces on floors.
   - Raise food and water bowls if your dog appears in pain and lowers her head when her bowl is on the floor.
   - Use ramps where needed
   - Talk to your vet about special food, medications, and supplements. Explore ancillary treatments,

like physical therapy, massage, acupuncture, Reiki, cold laser and others.

For most chronic conditions, you and your vet should choose the optimal pain management for your dog as her condition progresses. Pain medications may be selected by your vet specifically for your dog's breed, age and condition. Tell your vet about any "over the counter" drugs or supplements you are giving your dog. Never borrow medications from others without your vet's knowledge. Be ready to try new therapies and work with your vet by observing your dog at home and reporting any improvement or side effects.

How Pain Medication Works

Non-steroidal anti-inflammatory drugs (NSAIDs) act as pain relievers by reducing inflammation. The most commonly prescribed NSAIDs include:

- o Carprofen (Rimadyl)
- o Derocoxib (Deramaxx)
- o Firocoxib (Previcox)
- o Meloxicam (Metacam)
- o Robinacoxib (Onsior)
- o Other non-NSAID pain relievers include two "add-on" drugs:
  - • Gabapentin (Neurontin) is effective for chronic nerve pain

- Amantadine is usually used as an anti-viral drug and an amplifier for the pain relieving effects of NSAIDS

All NSAIDS can lead to gastrointestinal side effects and should be administered with food. If your dog experiences diarrhea, vomiting or a decrease in appetite, your vet may suggest reducing the dose, giving GI protectants or choosing a different drug. That way your dog can still benefit from the anti-inflammatory effect of NSAIDs without suffering significantly from harmful side effects. Do not use human NSAIDS such as Advil (Ibuprofen) or Aleve (Naproxen) for your dog.

Opioid pain relievers work by reducing the perception of pain in the brain. The most commonly used in veterinary medicine are:

- Tramadol
- Buprenorphine and Butorphanol
- Codeine. If used closely under a vet's guidance, Tylenol can sometimes be added.
- Hydrocodone or Oxycodone in association with surgery
- Transdermal Fentanyl or "pain patch" or Recuvyral
- Methadone

Human Medications Unsafe for Dogs

The following list is not complete, but it includes common drugs that are found in many households. These drugs should not be given to dogs:

o   Ibuprofen
o   Aleve
o   Tylenol (unless carefully prescribed by your vet)
o   Xanax
o   Adderall
o   Cymbalta

Giving Medication to Your Dog

You can mix medicine with your dog's food, but make sure she actually eats the medication. Wrapping a pill in a tasty slice of cheese, a dollop of cream cheese or peanut butter, or pill pockets can work well for some dogs. As Mary Poppins might have said during her dog-sitting years, a spoon full of peanut butter makes the medicine go down!

Just like children who don't want to take their medicine, after a while your dog might see through the ruse of hiding medication in food. In this case, your vet or vet tech can show you how to "pill" your dog. This involves placing the pill far back into your dog's throat, removing your hand quickly, closing her mouth and then stroking her throat to stimulate her salivary gland. When she licks toward her nose, you know she has swallowed the pill.

Some medications can be ground into a powder and mixed with water or compounded into a liquid form and squirted down your dog's throat. When squirting liquid into your dog's mouth, always be careful not to squirt too much. Make sure her head is not titled back, or she may choke on the liquid.

The Human Touch

You will probably know when your dog is suffering and when his suffering becomes intolerable. There may be times during palliative care when you cannot provide relief with medicine alone.

When one of our dogs was close to the end and in uncontrollable pain, we would lie near her, hold her lightly and sing her a soft song. She would lay her head down, her breathing would slow, her body relax, and she would close her eyes. When the song was done, she would open her eyes as if to ask for more. One day, we sang to her and held her for the last time as our veterinarian gave her an injection. She grew still, free of pain at last.

We all know what a dog can give to us. We are not always so aware of what we can give back. For many dogs, nothing is as vital as the human touch.

RESOURCES

○   American Veterinary Medical Association. (n.d.). Senior pet care. *American Veterinary Medical Association.* Retrieved from: https://www.avma.org/public/PetCare/Pages/Caring-for-an-Older-Pet-FAQs.aspx

○   Nicholas, J. (2014). How can I tell if my dog is in pain? *Preventive Vet.* Retrieved from:

http://www.preventivevet.com/dogs/how-can-i-tell-if-my-dog-is-in-pain

o University of California, San Diego Center for Integrative Medicine. (n.d.). How acupuncture can relieve pain and improve sleep, digestion and emotional well-being. *University of California, San Diego Center for Integrative Medicine.* Retrieved from: http://cim.ucsd.edu/clinical-care/acupuncture.shtml.

o U.S. Food and Drug Administration. (2016). Get the facts about pain relievers for pets. *U.S. Food and Drug Administration.* Retrieved from: http://www.fda.gov/AnimalVeterinary/ResourcesforYou/AnimalHealthLiteracy/ucm392732.html

PUCK

When he was nine, my beautiful golden retriever Puck developed a prolonged episode of vomiting and diarrhea. At first, I thought it might have been caused by eating too many oak leaves in our backyard. As poor Puck's discomfort continued, the vet suggested I bring him in for blood tests.

I was stunned when the tests came back with the suggestion of a lymphoproliferative cancer. It knocked me for a loop. There were lots of tears, anger, shock and deep sadness as I faced the prospect of losing my best friend.

The good news, fortunately, was that the course of the illness was likely to be long. After seeing the oncologist and understanding that I might still have a year or two together with Puck, I settled down. I had so many concerns about the road ahead – what would this process entail? What could I do to preserve Puck's playfulness and exuberance for as long as possible?

I tried to curb my hyper-vigilance – watching everything Puck did to make sure he was all right. But I kept reminding myself of the preciousness of the time I still had with him. I gave him special treats, took lots of walks and spent a lot of time playing with his tennis ball.

Then, things took a sudden turn for the worse. Puck developed a sudden nosebleed that turned out to be a nasal tumor. Although he now had trouble breathing through one side of his nose, Puck remained exuberant, was eating well and did not seem in pain. After several inconclusive biopsies, the vets conducted a CAT scan accompanied by a biopsy to plan for radiation. Although we were optimistic about palliation for his nasal tumor, he began to bleed and died suddenly that afternoon.

I learned afterwards that Puck's cancer had spread throughout his body. Aside from the shock and grief from his sudden death, I wondered how he was able to seem so well during his final weeks. Puck had gallantly faced his final days with such great courage, emotionally and physically. I loved him and knew that I had given that brave dog the extra care he so deserved.

−Linda B.

BEHAVIORAL CHANGES

Old age and life-threatening disease may be accompanied by changes in your dog's behavior, ranging from the obvious – lower energy, excessive sleeping, change in eating patterns, increased discomfort – to the more unsettling and profound.

COGNITIVE DYSFUNCTION

Like people, many dogs decline cognitively as they age. These changes result from neurodegenerative processes in the brain and may manifest behaviorally. In fact, among dogs 11–12 years old, 19 percent will manifest cognitive issues. Among dogs aged 15 to 16 years, the percentage soars to almost half (47 percent). These changes tend to be progressive. The diagnosis of cognitive dysfunction by your vet is often one of exclusion and should not be made until other causes are ruled out.

Cognitive dysfunction syndrome (CDS) consists of "disorientation, altered interactions with people or other pets, disruption of the sleep-wake cycle, house soiling, and altered activity level."

Dogs with cognitive issues can become disoriented or confused about their surroundings. It might seem like they forgot their previous training. They may have difficulty locating the door to go out or even get lost in their own house or in other familiar surroundings. They may stare into space or at a wall. They can seem less connected to people and at times, they can even appear not to recognize their owner. They appear anxious and pace around in a confused manner, are far less energetic and less willing to engage in usual activities.

Some dogs with CDS become incontinent, have difficulty sleeping or manifest a disruption of the usual sleep-wake cycle. Others may develop new fears and manifest behavioral changes such as anxiety, phobias, compulsive and repetitive behaviors or destructiveness. In some dogs, dementia is complicated by hearing or vision loss, which only increases the dog's general confusion. It is important for the owner to be aware of when these changes began and to consult your vet.

Other stressors in the dog's life will affect his behavior, especially those that disrupt his usual routine. These behaviors must be considered when evaluating how to manage your pet.

What You Can Do About Behavioral Change

o   Talk to your vet and assess the cause of your dog's behavioral changes.

o   Maintain your dog's routine schedule so he will know what to expect.

o   Make accommodations for his confusion.

o   Talk with your vet about using dementia drugs (Anipryl–Pfizer Animal Health; Selegiline) or drugs to reduce anxiety.

o   Try a senior diet with antioxidants, essential fatty acids, and mitochondrial cofactors.

BEHAVIOR PROBLEMS

If a dog's behavior changes as he gets older, it can be very distressing for the pet owner. Consult your vet to identify any medical conditions that account for the behavior. Providing a complete history of the nature, onset and course of the behavior is essential. In older dogs it is essential to rule out medical problems that may be treatable. For pets with behavioral problems, the treatment modalities are like those for younger dogs. However, because of the aging process, senior dogs may not be as responsive to some of the interventions.

The most common behavioral issues in older dogs include:
- Separation anxiety
- Fears and phobias
- Destructive behavior
- Aggression towards people or other animals
- Excessive vocalizations
- House soiling

These problems are often due to fear or painful medical problems. Always discuss these problems with your vet before deciding whether the changes are behavioral. In addition to understanding the causes, it is important to work out a treatment plan to reduce your dog's distress. This could include medication if anxiety and fear are actively contributing to the behaviors.

SEPARATION ANXIETY

Separation anxiety manifests as distress when a dog is separated from her favorite human or animal companion. It can even occur when your dog is simply anticipating a separation. This may emerge if there is a change in the dog's routine. Older dogs may have more trouble with any separation from their owners. Sometimes the distress escalates to severe anxiety, fear and even panic, but its emotional and behavioral manifestations may vary from dog to dog. The dog's usual coping mechanisms seem to fail, and she overreacts to the potential loss.

The most common symptoms of separation anxiety are vocalizations, inappropriate elimination and destructiveness. Dogs can become agitated at times, and at other times subdued or even depressed. Occasionally, a dog will exhibit her distress by incessant licking and self-grooming. Predisposing factors include early traumatic experiences, inexperience being alone, long pet owner departures, changes in routines, owner's anxiety about leaving and underlying medical or cognitive problems in older dogs.

How You Can Decrease Separation Anxiety

o Mix it up a little – change predictable departure routines that precipitate the anxiety.

o Create a new routine around departures. Try taking your dog on a long walk before you leave. This will give her some extra time with you before you go and will tire her out. Both can help ease the transition between your being there and her being alone.

o Provide a chew toy before you leave. This can be a fun distraction that can help "change the subject" for her.

o Remain calm when you leave. Say goodbye in a low-key way. Remember, your dog knows you pretty well. If you're nervous about leaving her alone, she'll pick up on that.

o Play music or leave the TV on to keep her company, tuned to something relaxing on the nerves – no 24-hour news channels!

o Confine your dog to a smaller space in your home. Less space to roam can make her feel more secure.

o Consider medication after talking with your vet if nothing else works.

o Separation anxiety in some dogs may actually improve as they get older. They sleep more, may not hear well and may find the time alone quite peaceful. They may not even notice that you have left.

AGGRESSION

Aggression Toward People

Most often, the onset of aggression towards people by older dogs is due either to fear or painful medical conditions, such as osteoarthritis or dental problems. This may be compounded by a decrease in hearing, sight, and mobility that makes the dog more helpless and frightened.

If you dog seems to be getting more aggressive, keep a closer eye on her interactions with strangers, visitors and children. If you notice that your dog is showing signs of stress or is fearful, remove her from the situation. Signs of stress or fear include panting, trembling, agitation, putting her ears back and tucking her tail in, wagging her tail low or hiding. Fearful aggression may be hard to treat, but desensitization and counterconditioning have been used successfully, even in older dogs.

Less commonly, an older dog's aggression may be dominance-related. In this situation, the owner must assert his dominant position in a kind and compassionate manner. Obedience exercises, head collars and even basket muzzles can be used.

Aggression Towards Other Dogs

Aggression towards other dogs can happen when multiple dogs live together. There is a hierarchy, with one dog as the dominant leader. Often, the dominant dog is the one who was there first. As dogs age and a younger dog matures, he may challenge the dominant dog for position, especially if the older dog becomes less assertive, sicker, and weaker.

If the dogs vary in size, the smaller dog may get hurt. The senior dog may have to relinquish his position and if he is unwilling, serious injury might occur. As the owner, you should support the dominant dog in his position, but there may be discretion about which dog to choose. Your vet or a behavioral specialist will be able to help you sort this out.

Another way the balance of doggie power can change is when a new puppy is brought into the home. Puppies are energetic, playful, exuberant and sometimes out of control. These behaviors are often annoying to an elderly dog who may try to give the puppy a message with nips and barks. If the puppy doesn't respond appropriately, the older dog might become even more aggressive. Before this happens, you should intervene and monitor their interactions. You might have to provide a separate place for the puppy to play, leash the puppy if necessary at times, provide distractions and give the little fellow some obedience exercises.

One of our old, but still feisty, Golden Retrievers developed cancer. Although he was completely loving with people, he could be aggressive and even dangerous with other dogs. Bringing him to the groomer or to the vet was always a challenge that caused us considerable anxiety (not to mention the other dogs). We had to muzzle him, clear out the waiting room and keep him away from other dogs. Due to his cancer, we needed to visit the vet oncologist every eight weeks. The waiting room was an ordeal, but one we were ready to take on.

The only way to groom him was to bring him after hours – which always had to be planned some months ahead. Although mobile groomers were available, none were willing to deal with a 75-pound dog in their truck. So, we worked out an alternative with our vet tech from the animal hospital. She came to our house and we groomed him at home. She would bathe him on a warm day in the backyard, cut his hair short, and trim his nails. It was a challenge, but he always felt and looked better afterwards.

Pet owners facing similar challenges should learn about the Fear Free Initiative (www.fearfreepets.com), an innovative movement developed by Dr. Marty Becker. In his words, "take the pet out of 'petrified' during veterinary visits." This begins with the first vet visit by using techniques to comfort and encourage the dog's cooperation.

Excessive Vocalization

Elderly dogs are very sensitive to changes in routine and separations. They will express their distress by excessive barking, howling or whimpering. This may be compounded if your dog also has compromised cognition. Sometimes, your dog's vocalizing may be an attempt to get more attention or it may be induced by fear.

Dogs who are isolated at home are more likely to try to get your attention. Keep in mind there are many different reasons why your dog might be vocalizing his discomfort. Your response can be as varied as the situations causing the problem. Regardless of the reason, patience is the key.

Remember, your dog is distressed and can't tell you why. If you were in his situation, you would feel aggravated too. Patience and understanding in large doses will go a long way in reducing your dog's stress – and yours!

House Soiling

Inappropriate defecation is actually less common than some of the other behavioral problems described above. It may be a manifestation of a behavioral problem in an older dog, but more often is just a symptom of the aging process.

RESOURCES

Behavior Problems

o **Nylabone. (n.d.).** *Tips for solving common behavior problems*. **Retrieved from:** https://www.nylabone.com/dog101/tips-for-solving-common-behavior-problems.

o **Becker, M. (n.d.). Fear Free Initiative. Retrieved from:** www.fearfreepets.com.

Gear: Behavior Problems

- o Adaptil Adjustable Calming Dog Collar. Available at: www.adaptil.com/us/.

- o Sentry PetCare Calming Collar for Dogs. Available at: www.sentrypetcare.com.

- o Thundershirt for Dogs. Available at: www.thundershirt.com.

ISABELLA

After struggling through the first couple of frightening seizures that our Spinoni started having in the first years of her life, we learned to stay calm and help Isabella through them.

My mother worked in a hospital and told us about something that she would do for children who looked like they were going to have a seizure. She would rub their temples and it would stop or shorten the seizure. When we noticed a seizure coming on with Isabella, we tried the same thing and it worked!

This did not end the seizures completely, but it did limit the severity of some of them. By getting more comfortable with witnessing and managing her seizures, we were able to help Isabella live as healthy life as possible to the age of 14.

—Vincent S.

SEIZURES

Canine seizures are the most commonly occurring neurological problem in animal hospitals. Recurrent seizures are referred to as epilepsy. Seizures reflect an abnormal discharge of electrical activity in the brain and can manifest as loss of consciousness, involuntary muscle movements, behavioral changes, or autonomic discharge like salivation, urination and defecation.

In younger dogs between the ages of 6 months and 6 years, seizures are often idiopathic, or without an identifiable cause.

A seizure may reflect an underlying health problem that is sometimes serious and should always be evaluated by a vet.

Seizures are certainly frightening for the owner, too. Most owners feel helpless and worried about how much the dog is suffering. After a seizure, a dog may be extremely tired, disconnected from the environment, and not seem to know where he is.

If the seizures are frequent, the idea of euthanizing naturally enters your mind. Is this it? Has my dog reached his time? However, euthanasia may be premature. Effective medical management techniques can really help in controlling seizures. Have an open discussion with your vet to understand the nature of seizure disorders and what can be done to help your dog.

Seizures can be divided into three phases:

Pre-Ictal

In the period before a seizure, dogs may experience strange feelings or behaviors known as "auras" which are a warning sign before the seizure occurs. Your dog may appear anxious, fearful, agitated or spacey. These symptoms may herald the beginning of a seizure.

Ictal

This is the actual seizure during which a dog may lose consciousness, pee or defecate, and have abnormal uncontrolled movements of her limbs. These may represent grand mal convulsions, or the seizure may be petit mal characterized by brief and sudden loss of attention. Petit mal seizures are more limited and focal, may only involve one side of the dog's body, or may be as minimal as the dog looking "spaced out" and distracted. Other signs that a dog is having a seizure are sudden licking of odd objects or biting at imaginary flies.

Post-Ictal

This phase varies from dog to dog and from seizure to seizure, ranging from a few minutes to several days. Your dog may seem overly tired and distracted. Some dogs experience temporary blindness, excessive drooling or aggression.

Regardless of the nature of the seizure, try to remain calm, stay near your dog and keep her safe. If the seizure occurs near a stairway, try to block the area so your dog can't fall down the stairs or be injured. Be reassuring to your dog, but do not put your hands or fingers in or near his mouth.

It is important for you to try to estimate the length of the seizure, so you can report this to your vet. Most seizures last from seconds to two minutes. If seizures are continuous or last up to 3 to 5 minutes, take your dog to an animal hospital emergency room immediately. During a seizure, a dog's temperature may rise to unacceptable heights, causing damage to neurons in his brain.

In the event of a seizure, bring your pet to the vet during the attack or as soon as possible after it ends. Seizures are more easily treated when they are a relatively new symptom than if they have been occurring for a long while. Balancing the choice and dosage of medication with potential side effects is very important.

A realistic goal is to reduce the seizures by at least half and to help the pet owner feel more confident and comfortable at managing the seizures. Treating the seizure medically often results in a better quality of life for your dog and your family.

Guidelines for Mandatory Medical Treatment

After the first seizure, be sure to contact your vet. Pursue medical treatment if the following situations occur:

o   Seizures resulting from trauma, a known illness (e.g., tumor) or a toxin

o   When a seizure lasts longer than 3 minutes

o   Multiple seizures in a short period (e.g., cluster seizures)

o   Increased number of seizures

o   Prolonged after effects

Sometimes seizures are infrequent, brief, and recovery is rapid. In these cases, medical treatment may not be necessary. Even if the seizures occur less frequently (4 to 6 weeks apart), treatment is highly recommended if they pose a likelihood of injury to the dog, extremely stress the dog owner or result in frequent ER visits with thoughts of euthanizing the dog.

Realistic Expectations Can Help You Deal with Seizures

o   The seizures may not go away entirely. The goal should be to reduce them to a level that allows for the dog's best quality of life.

o   Antiepileptic treatment is lifelong.

o   Many dogs experience adverse effects from the medications.

o   The pet owner should be committed to a systematic plan for managing the seizures that includes administering medications at specific times.

o   Plans for cluster seizures should include emergency treatment at home.

o   The dog will need medication and periodic evaluations that might be costly.

o   The pet owner must make a genuine commitment to caring for a dog with seizures.

Complementary or alternative medicines are sometimes used to help treat epileptic seizures in dogs. The results have been variable. These therapies include acupuncture, ketogenic diet, and herbal and plant-based remedies. If these are being considered, be sure to discuss them first with your vet.

BÊTE NOIRE

The hardest thing is deciding the "right time" to end a sick or elderly dog's life. They can't tell us when they've had enough, but sometimes they don't have to.

At age 11, my American Staffordshire Terrier was diagnosed with lymphoma. A local canine oncologist kept her alive and comfortable on oral chemotherapy for sixteen months, but Bête's condition rapidly declined in her 13th year. Tumors were ravaging her system.

One cold March morning, she went outside like usual, but soon lay down in the snow and refused to return inside. I insisted she do so, but she immediately asked to go out again and returned to lie in the same spot on the sloping hill, head up, gazing across the snowy fields.

I called a dog-whisperer friend who told us, "She's telling you it's time." By then, I had convinced Bête to curl up in a nest of blankets on the porch – a chilly bed, but at least a dry one.

She lay there patiently, but mostly unresponsive, until the vet tech arrived to help ease her out of pain for good.

–Marjorie K.

PART III
AT THE END

Bringing a dog into your home is a decision with long-term implications. Since a dog's life is relatively short, adoption is a deep commitment to stay with him as he grows into an adult and, eventually, into his geriatric years. If you adopt an older dog, your time together is even shorter.

It's difficult to imagine your frisky, playful, mischievous puppy as a senior citizen – with many of the ailments that beset all of us as we grow old. Although we all know that bringing a dog into our home will ultimately result in loss, most of us don't think about the end until there is an immediate reason to face the inevitable.

Often, we often do not fully consider how the canine life cycle will unfold or what it will entail as our dog ages. There are no nursing homes or assisted living facilities for dogs. You are it!

As caretakers, our job is to ease our beloved dogs into the end of life as much as possible by limiting suffering and supporting a reasonable quality of life for as long as is humane and tolerable.

After we have done all we can for our dog, how do we know when it is time to say goodbye? We can't ask our dog directly, but with support from a veterinarian and a deep personal commitment and love for our dog, you can get it about right.

WHEN IS IT "TIME"?

Deciding when is the hardest part of seeing your dog through to the end and it can be an agonizing decision. You want to keep his life going, but you also want to do the right thing for him.

We see this as balancing an equation between his quality of life, and his suffering and pain. But people view quality of life in many different ways, depending on their values and beliefs. The level of suffering may be very hard to assess. Of course, our views are strongly influenced by our loving relationship with our dog, his place in our heart and the anticipation of losing him.

Assessing Your Dog's Quality of Life

According to bioethicist Jessica Pierce, assessing a dog's quality of life (QOL) is central to the process of providing end-of-life palliative care. She defines this process as considering "how an animal's physical, emotional, and social well-being is affected by disease, disability, or changes related to advanced age." Various frameworks and tools that support an assessment are increasingly available to both veterinarians and to dog owners for use at home. However, none alone can be considered a "gold standard." Each QOL assessment approach has strengths and weaknesses. Over time, these tools may evolve into a few very useful instruments.

Pierce stresses that an effective QOL assessment should include a sense of how the dog is experiencing its own circumstances. Pain, suffering and mobility might seem paramount to humans, but dogs may have a wide range of coping strategies. She suggests tracking a dog's "positive" and "negative" emotional states. Below are some experiences that may be positive or negative to a dog. Keep in mind: all dogs are different. Only close observation, attuned to the dog's moods, will yield useful information for making end-of-life decisions.

Positive Experiences:
Sensory and mental stimulation
Companionship
Good food
Comfortable bedding
Playtime

Control over oneself and environment

Negative Experiences

Pain	Dehydration
Nausea	Social isolation
Lack of appetite	Confusion
Trouble breathing	Agitation/Anxiety
Loss of mobility	Boredom/Depression
Incontinence	Fear

Adapted from Shannon, Pierce, and Shearer (2017)

A Quality of Life Scale developed by veterinarian Dr. Alice Villalobos assesses seven criteria related to a dog's quality of life. This is a helpful tool for dog owners to use at home, but it's not definitive. Instead, it should be used as a way to help think about the decision you are faced with. Always consult a veterinarian about your and your dog's specific situation before moving forward with any major decision regarding end-of-life care.

The HHHHHMM Scale breaks down your dog's state into seven categories: Hurt, Hunger, Hydration, Hygiene, Happiness, Mobility, and More good days than bad. Each of the seven categories are treated with equal weight, then used to compile an overall score to determine quality of life. As you assess your dog's QOL, always give extra weight to issues such as cessation of eating or drinking, difficulty walking or getting up, or severe spasms or seizures as indicators of prolonged extreme pain or potential physical collapse. Most importantly, it is never acceptable for your dog to be unable to breathe properly; this must be addressed by a veterinarian as quickly as possible.

Use the scale as needed – weekly, daily, hourly. A total score of 70 means that your dog's quality of life is very good. The lower the score, the worse the quality of life. A score over 5 in each category is an acceptable number. If the overall score is below 35, discuss options for palliative care that may improve the score by at least 30 to 50 percent. Improvement is the goal. If that is not possible, then it may be time to discuss hospice care and euthanasia with your vet.

The Quality of Life Scale	
Score	Criterion
0-10	**HURT** - Adequate pain control and breathing ability are of the utmost concern. If the pet can't breathe properly, nothing else matters. Is oxygen supplementation necessary? Is the pet's pain well managed?
0-10	**HUNGER** - Is the pet eating enough? Does hand feeding help? Does the pet need a feeding tube?
0-10	**HYDRATION** - Is the pet dehydrated? For patients not drinking enough, use subcutaneous fluids daily to supplement fluid intake.
0-10	**HYGIENE** - The pet should be brushed and cleaned, particularly after eliminations. Avoid sores with soft bedding and keep all wounds clean.
0-10	**HAPPINESS** - Does the pet express joy and interest? Is the pet responsive to family, toys, etc.? Is the pet depressed, lonely, anxious, bored or afraid? Can the pet's bed be moved to be close to family activities?
0-10	**MOBILITY** - Can the pet get up without assistance? Does the pet need human or mechanical help (e.g., a cart)? Does the dog feel like going for a walk? Is the pet having seizures or stumbling? (Some feel that euthanasia is preferable to amputation, but an animal with limited mobility yet still alert and responsive, can have a good quality of life if the family is committed to helping their pet.)
0-10	**MORE GOOD DAYS THAN BAD** - When bad days outnumber good days, quality of life might be too compromised. When a healthy human-animal bond is no longer possible, the end is near. The decision for euthanasia needs to be made if the pet is suffering. It is ideal when a pet's death comes peacefully and painlessly at home.
TOTAL	A total over 35 points represents acceptable life quality to continue with pet hospice (Pawspice).

Original concept, *Oncology Outlook*, by Dr. Alice Villalobos, *Quality of Life Scale Helps Make Final Call*, VPN, 09/2004; formatted for *Canine and Feline Geriatric Oncology: Honoring the Human-Animal Bond*, Blackwell Publishing, 2007. Adapted for2011 IVAPM Hospice Statement, 2013 SVME on line Ethics Course, and the NAP Spring Forum 2015. Reprinted in *Canine and Feline Anesthesia, Co-Existing Disease*, Nova Publications, etc., with permission.

IS IT THE END?

The end of your dog's life may be quiet or catastrophic. You may need to call or visit a vet. You will likely feel confused, helpless, very sad and a little scared. None of this is avoidable. It is part of the territory between life and death. You may not be completely sure of what is right or wrong, but don't be afraid to make a decision and take action. You are acting out of love for your dog, just as you always have, and that is the best you can do. Alicia Karas DVM, who heads the Tufts Pet Loss Hotline, emphasized that "when to euthanize is a very deeply spiritual decision."

More often than not, your dog will let you know when it's time to let go. Then, your decision to euthanize will be the most humane approach. It ends pain and suffering that should no longer be endured. You must have the courage and selflessness to take this final step.

Euthanasia can be carried out at an animal hospital or clinic, or at your home. Some owners prefer the home environment because hospitals and clinics can be fearful settings for many dogs in contrast to the familiarity and comfort of home. This is a decision you need to make in a way that works for your dog, for you and for your family. There is no right or wrong way to do this as long as your dog is as comfortable as possible.

The euthanasia procedure usually involves two steps. First, your vet injects a calming sedative that causes your dog to relax and drift into unconsciousness. Second, your vet injects a lethal dose of pentobarbital adjusted for your dog's weight.

The drug may be given intravenously or by another method to avoid the stress and strain of locating a vein.

Your dog's motion and breathing will slow down rapidly, and then he will quietly pass away in a minute or two. Some owners want to be by their dog's side, calming and petting him as he drifts away. Others do not. This is a decision you need to make for yourself. Whatever you decide will be the right choice.

Once your dog has passed away, you must decide what to do with his body. The options generally include burial at a pet cemetery or cremation with return of the remains in an urn. Talk with your vet about the options available.

Dealing with Grief

Saying goodbye to your dog often begins well before the final moments. Once you realize that your beloved pet is declining, has an untreatable disease or is just very old, you have begun the painful process of saying goodbye. At the same time, you can value and enjoy the remaining days you have together.

Anticipatory grief is part of the grieving process and may be as intense as or more intense than the actual feelings of loss itself. Not everyone experiences anticipation of the loss, but when they do it takes many forms and echoes the feelings you may have when your dog eventually passes away.

Although denial may obscure many painful feelings, avoidance of your dog's approaching death may interfere with the many ways you can relieve your dog's suffering and possibly even prolong his life. However, for some people, denial may actually help them cope with overwhelming feelings about the inevitable outcome and can enable them to do what is necessary to support their dog.

As part of this process, it is important to consider what you and your family can tolerate and manage. Of course, as very committed dog owners, this may be a time to face some of your own demons, prejudices and challenges. It may be a time to work through some of your own feelings about loss. You may find that you are able to take on more than you imagine.

Grieving is a dynamic and complex emotional experience. It takes many forms and occurs over varying periods of time. Imagining the loss of your friend is heartbreaking, but it is inevitable when you take on the responsibilities of owning a dog. Sadness is painful, but it is part of all our lives.

Balance the sadness with the joy you have experienced with your dog, and all the ways you have loved and supported each other. These feelings can sit side by side. Cry when you need to. Be angry. Be compassionate toward yourself. Talk to others – and your dog – about how much you will miss him. Spend more time with him and enjoy whatever you are able to do together.

The loss of your dog may bring up unresolved feelings about losses of other pets, friends, and family members. Painful, yes, but an opportunity to work through feelings about those other losses, and perhaps get some closure. Think of it as another gift your dog is giving you.

Elisabeth Kubler-Ross brought death out of the closet, encouraging us to talk about the inevitable losses that are part of all our lives. She described five stages of grief – denial, anger, bargaining, depression and, finally, acceptance. Although often misinterpreted as discrete stages that people go through in a linear fashion, these stages actually overlap, and are not necessarily always fully experienced.

Everyone goes through grief differently and according to their own personal experience. Intense feelings may accompany these "stages" and can take many forms. Sometimes, feelings of grief come in waves over long periods and may often be triggered by reminders of your lost pet. People have good and bad days accompanied by a range of different feelings. With grief, anything goes.

You may be numb, or it might not hit you until months later. Don't let that confuse you or compound your grief with guilt. "Why don't I feel sadder?" This is perfectly normal.

You may experience strong feelings of grief and loss that can surprise you with their intensity. Whatever happens to you, it is best to take it head on and not avoid or deny your grief. If you face it and let it move through you, you will heal over time.

You may be surprised to find yourself in tears at reminders of your lost companion – go ahead, cry it out and it will pass until the next time. Sometimes, it may feel that you will just cry forever, but sadness has its own cycle. When expressed, it usually ends with you feeling better. Bottled up feelings sit heavily in your body and soul and can interfere with the healing process.

Sorrow is most often compartmentalized and lives on a different channel – often not interfering with our capacity to experience happiness and joy. We can be sad for our loss, but happy for our fond memories of all the good times we had with our pet.

The circumstances surrounding a dog's death will shape the grieving process. A sudden loss may feel catastrophic. You may have little to no time for reflection on what it will be like to live without your dog and to process the complicated feelings that the death evokes. This type of loss may take more time to work through. Unexpected death can feel overwhelming. Be sure to give yourself time to integrate the loss, understand that unexpected events can, with time, be processed and managed. You may feel intensely vulnerable and disorganized at first, but be kind to yourself, stay with these feelings. Let time do its job. Give yourself the time you need to integrate the enormity of your loss.

Over time, the rawness of the feelings will dissipate and transform into fond memories and warm feelings. Be kind and compassionate to yourself when you are dealing with the pain of your loss.

Do not hesitate to reach out to family, friends or your vet to share your thoughts and feelings. It can feel good to talk to other dog owners who have lost their beloved pets and share your experiences. Eventually, your grief will soften.

Many resources are available to support you through the grieving process and the impact of euthanasia on you and your family. In addition to taking care of yourself and providing intermittent periods of rest, it is important to build support from people close to you. Other important resources include pet loss support hotlines, animal support groups, grief counselors, and your vet.

Talking with Children

For many children, the death of a pet is their very first experience with loss. Carefully consider how your children will respond and what the dog has meant to each child. You should consider your child's age, developmental stage, temperament and any special challenges they may have.

In general, we believe that children should be told the truth of the dog's condition and be included in the grieving process. It will help them accept the natural life cycle that all of us must face and can be an important emotional learning experience.

It is important to tell your child the truth about what happened to your dog, and not make up stories about the dog being sent to a farm, running away or going to sleep forever. You can omit gruesome and disturbing details but be honest and always tell the truth about your dog's death.

It is important to answer questions your child may have and to be aware that they will feel the dog's absence no matter how young. Be there for them. Encourage children to share their feelings and to express their sadness, anger, sense of loss, and loneliness. You might look at photographs, draw pictures together or reminisce about the many good times you all shared. Creating a memorial or a funeral ritual around the loss may also be helpful to children.

Remembering Your Dog

Losing a beloved dog can be traumatic. Create ways to remember your dog that are meaningful for you and your family. Memorialize her by planting a tree in your backyard and attaching a plaque to it. Frame and hang up photos. Some owners have a painting done from a photograph. If you are artistic, paint your dog yourself. If your dog is cremated, you might want to spread her ashes in some favorite places or in your own backyard. You can find a beautiful urn to contain the ashes and put your dog's name on it.

Have a conversation with older children to find out what would be helpful for them. There are many ways for a family to create a farewell ritual in which the children are involved.

The playwright Eugene O'Neill helped his wife cope with the loss of their dog by crafting a "Last Will & Testament" in the dog's voice that has given a smile and a tear to many dog owners who are grappling with those awful moments. An excerpt is reprinted here:

"The Last Will & Testament of Silverdene Emblem O'Neill"

I, SILVERDENE EMBLEM O'NEILL (familiarly known to my family, friends, and acquaintances as Blemie), because the burden of my years and infirmities is heavy upon me, and I realize the end of my life is near, do hereby bury my last will and testament in the mind of my Master. He will not know it is there until after I am dead.

I have little in the way of material things to leave. Dogs are wiser than men. They do not set great store upon things. They do not waste their days hoarding property. They do not ruin their sleep worrying about how to keep the objects they have, and to obtain the objects they have not. There is nothing of value I have to bequeath except my love and my faith.

I ask my Master and Mistress to remember me always, but not to grieve for me too long. In my life I have tried to be a comfort to them in time of sorrow, and a reason for added joy in their happiness. Dogs do not fear death as men do. We accept it as part of life, not as something alien and terrible which destroys life. What may come after death, who knows? I am afraid this is too much for even such a dog as I am to expect. But peace, at least, is certain. Peace and long rest for weary old heart and head and limbs, and eternal sleep in the earth I have loved so well.

One last request I earnestly make. I have heard my Mistress say, "When Blemie dies we must never have another dog. I love him so much I could never love another one." Now I would ask her, for love of me, to have another. It would be a poor tribute to my memory never to have a dog again. What I would like to feel is that, having once had me in the family, now she cannot live without a dog!

One last word of farewell, Dear Master and Mistress. Whenever you visit my grave, say to yourselves with regret but also with happiness in your hearts at the remembrance of my long happy life with you: "Here lies one who loved us and whom we loved." No matter how deep my sleep I shall hear you, and not all the power of death can keep my spirit from wagging a grateful tail.

Tao House, December 17th, 1940

POSTSCRIPT

We may never fully understand what bonds a dog and a human so closely, but somehow over time we come to mean more to each other than we could have imagined on that day when we first met.

We hope this book gives you the confidence and support to stand by your dog to extend and maximize the last chapter in your lives together. And we hope that your extra time together helps prepare you both to face the end with some resilience and celebration of the good times you have had with each other.

Someday when the time is right, you may bring another dog into your life. We always do.

KUMA

Kuma was a beautiful Mountain Cur who we rescued from a "kill" shelter. He came to us shortly after he was hit by a car and had surgery to remove his rear leg. He lived with us for 15 years. His disability never phased him. He approached everything he did with a positive "can do" attitude, and his love of life always outshone his disability, inspiring us all along the way.

As Kuma grew old, we could tell he was growing tired. His single rear leg had wallowed out of the hip socket and he became wobbly, unable to go much further than our yard. He struggled when climbing steps. We promised him that when the time came, we wouldn't let him suffer, but we told him he would have to let us know.

That time did come one morning when he wouldn't get up on his front legs. We blanket-carried him to the truck and rode to the vet. Lab and x-rays told us he had bone cancer and his liver was failing. The vet gave him an injection for pain and we could see the relief wash over him. When we asked about prognosis if they did everything possible, the vet said, "He's 95 years old. The prognosis is guarded."

With tears in our eyes, we laid on the floor with Kuma and whispered to him, "Yes, you've told us clearly and it's time to go." We held him while they started the IV, stroking him as the medicine took effect. Two minutes later, he was gone.

Losing Kuma is every bit as painful today as it was in that moment when we knew he'd left us forever. But we also knew that keeping him alive just because we would miss him would not be fair to him. Just one week after he passed, we received a Facebook post that two Mountain Cur puppies had been found abandoned on the side of the road. Emaciated, starving, full of worms and parasites, one died, but the other made it and needed a home.

Kumi came into our lives that day.

—Kez W.

ACKNOWLEDGMENTS

This book was a labor of love inspired by dogs who are now with us, those who have passed on, and those who will become future members of our families. They add immeasurably to our lives and teach us about unconditional love.

John Kellogg has been involved in every aspect of this book—its conception, writing, editing, graphic design, and publishing. Without his sage advice, diverse skills, and love of dogs, our book would not have been possible. We thank the dog lovers who contributed their heartfelt vignettes to show our readers what can be done. Christina Ean Spangler's (spanglerstudios.com) appealing graphics bring some lightness to this somber topic and beautifully illustrate the main points. Our thanks to Laurie Kaplan of JanGen Press for editing the final manuscript.

Dr. Alice Villalobos, a pioneer in palliative care of dogs, was kind enough to comment on our manuscript and write an inspiring foreword. Author and bioethicist Jessica Pierce helped us to improve the book considerably, most importantly by emphasizing how hospice and palliative care for dogs exists along a continuum of possibilities.

The hard work of dedicated nonprofit organizations to meet the needs of senior dogs and place them in permanent homes has enhanced the lives of many dogs who have found the love they deserve in their final years. We especially thank Lisa Lunghofer of Grey Muzzle Org and Michelle Nichols, Director of The Animal Hospice, End-of-Life and Palliative Care Project and 2018 President-Elect of the International Association of Animal Hospice and Palliative Care, for their support.

Finally, we thank Jennifer Bassuk and Larry Kirshbaum for their belief in our book. They helped connect us to Willow Street Press and Susan Konig, whose hard work has brought this project to fruition. We are grateful that each saw the uniqueness and usefulness of this book in supporting aging and ailing dogs, and the people who stand by them.

GENERAL REFERENCES

Borzendowski, J. (2007). *Caring for your aging dog: A quality of life guide for your dog's senior years.* New York, New York: Sterling Publishing Company.

Charleson, S. (2013). *The possibility dogs: What a handful of 'unadoptables' taught me about service, hope, and healing.* Boston: Houghton Mifflin Harcourt.

Cornell University College of Veterinary Medicine. *Pet loss support hotline.* Available at: https://www2.vet.cornell.edu/about-us/outreach/pet-loss-support-hotline.

Cummings School of Veterinary Medicine at Tufts University. *The newsletter for caring dog owners.* Available at www.tuftsyourdog.com.

Dodman, N. (2002). *If only they could speak: Stories about pets and their people.* New York, New York: W.W. Norton & Company.

Faculty of the Cummings School of Veterinary Medicine at Tufts University. (2012). *Good old dog: Expert advice for keeping your aging dog happy, healthy and comfortable.* N. Dodman (Ed.). New York, NY: Houghton Mifflin Harcourt.

Goldberg, K.J. (2016). Veterinary hospice and palliative care: A comprehensive review of the literature. *British Medical Journal,* 178(15), 369-374.

Kachnic, J. (2012). *Your dog's golden years: A manual for senior dog care.* Denver, CO: Wallingford Vale Publishing.

Koktavy, D. (2010). *The legacy of Beezer and Boomer: Lessons of living and dying from my canine brothers.* Denver, CO: B Brothers Press.

Kowalski, G. (2012). *Goodbye, friend: Healing wisdom for anyone who has ever lost a pet.* Novato, CA: New World Library.

Kubler-Ross, E., & Kessler, D. (2005). *On grief and grieving: Finding the meaning of grief through the five stages of loss.* New York, NY: Scribner.

Levinson, B. (1984). Grief at the loss of a pet. In W.J. Kay, H. Nieburg, A. Kutscher, et al. (Eds.), *Pet loss and human bereavement.* Ames, IA: Iowa State University Press.

Merck Manuals. *Veterinary manual.* Available at www.merckvetmanual.com.

Morgan, D. (2007). *The living well guide for senior dogs: Everything you need to know for a happy & healthy companion.* Neptune City, NJ: TFH Publications.

Nakaya, S.F. (2005). *Kindred spirit, kindred care: Making health decisions on behalf of our animal companions.* Novato, CA: New World Library.

National Academy of Sciences. (2009). *Recognition and alleviation of pain in laboratory animals.* Washington, DC: The National Academies Press. Retrieved from http://dels-old.nas.edu/animal_pain?dogs.shtml.

Pierce, J. (2012). *The last walk: Reflections on our pets at the end of their lives.* Chicago, IL: University of Chicago Press.

Pierce, J. (2016). *Run, spot, run: The ethics of keeping pets.* Chicago, IL: University of Chicago Press.

Sanders, S. (2015). *Seizures in dogs and cats.* Ames, IA: Wiley Blackwell.

Schaer, M., & Gaschen, F. (Eds.). (2016). *Clinical medicine of the dog and cat* (5th ed.). Boca Raton, FL: CRC Press.

Shanan, A., Pierce, J., Shearer, T. (2017) *Hospice and Palliative Care for Companion Animals.* Hoboken, NJ: John Wiley & Sons, Inc.

Shojai, A. (2011). *Complete care for your aging dog.* New York, NY: New American Library.

Stewart, G., Rainwater, D., & Rainwater, K. (2008). *When your best friend becomes your old friend: How to care for a geriatric canine.* CreateSpace Publishing.

Van de Poll, W. (2016). *My dog is dying: What do I do?* Center for Pet Loss Grief.

Villalobos, A., & Kaplan, L. (2017) *Canine and feline geriatric oncology: Honoring the human-animal bond* (2nd ed.). Ames, IA: Wiley Blackwell.

Wolfelt, A.D. (2004). *When your pet dies: A guide to mourning, remembering and healing.* Fort Collins, CO: Companion Press.

Tributes to Dogs: Stories, Poems, Insights

The Bark. (Eds.). (2003). *Dog is my co-pilot: Great writers on the world's oldest friendship.* New York, NY: Three Rivers Press.

Bekoff, M. (2007). *The emotional lives of animals: A leading scientist explores animal joy, sorrow, and empathy — and why they matter.* Novato, CA: New World Library.

Dewey, C., & da Costa, R.C. (2016). *Practical guide to canine and feline neurology.* Ames, IA: Wiley Blackwell.

Gilbert, M. (2014). *Off the leash: A year at the dog park.* New York, NY: St. Martin's Press.

Goodall, J., & Bekoff, M. (2002). *The ten trusts: What we must do to care for the animals we love.* San Francisco, CA: HarperCollins Publishers.

Homans, J. (2012). *What's a dog for?: The surprising history, science, philosophy and politics of man's best friend.* New York, NY: The Penguin Press.

Horowitz, A. (2009). *Inside of a dog: What dogs see, smell and know.* New York, NY: Scribner.

Hunt, L.E. (Ed.). (1998, 2000). *Angel pawprints: Reflections on loving and losing a canine companion.* Pasadena, CA: Darrowby

McElroy, S.C. (1996). *Animals as teachers and healers: True stories and reflections.* New York, NY: Ballantine Publishing Group.

McElroy, S.C. (2004). *All my relations: Living with animals as teachers and healers.* Novato, CA: New World Library.

Oliver, M. (2013). *Dog Songs.* New York, NY: The Penguin Press.

Stilwell, V. (2016). *The secret language of dogs: Unlocking the canine mind for a happier pet.* Berkeley, CA: Ten Speed Press.

ABOUT THE AUTHORS

Ellen L. Bassuk, M.D., is a distinguished researcher and advocate who has dedicated her life to understanding and ending family and child homelessness. For over 30 years, she has given a voice to the most marginalized families in our society. Ellen is a board-certified psychiatrist and an Associate Professor of Psychiatry at Harvard Medical School. "I've always had a dog at my side – sometimes two or three – and the love and support they give is like no other. But to love a dog is also to lose them, and that's when it's time for us to give back."

Julie Santoes is a high-energy veterinary technician who specialized for 15 years in providing home hospice care and euthanasia. She now practices in a full-service veterinary clinic in Massachusetts and continues to provide end-of-life home care for domestic animals. "I've been on the frontlines of pet care for more than 20 years. I'm still inspired every day by the compassion and caring I feel for animals and being their voice – especially when they are suffering."

Kate Pittman, D.V.M., has practiced as a "house call" veterinarian in Greater Boston for nearly 30 years. Trained at the Cummings School of Veterinary Medicine at Tufts University, she views veterinary care as including not only the technical aspects of treating illness but caring for the whole pet and the family around it as well – a practice especially suited to pets in their senior years. Kate brings her expertise with ailing or aging dogs to this book particularly in areas of pain management, mobility and medication.

Christina Ean Spangler is a graduate of Rhode Island School of Design, and after exploring a career as a stop-motion animator for children's television and commercials, she now works as a freelance illustrator. "I grew up in a home with pets, including cats and dogs, and have many cherished memories of them. I thoroughly enjoyed being a part of the collaborative effort for this book."
www.spanglerstudios.com.

CPSIA information can be obtained
at www.ICGtesting.com
Printed in the USA
LVHW041208300619
622775LV00002B/253

9 780997 831658